100 WA...
Yorkshire (western)

The Crowood Press

First published in 1991 by
The Crowood Press Ltd
Ramsbury, Marlborough
Wiltshire SN8 2HR

New edition 1996

© The Crowood Press Ltd 1991

British Library Cataloguing in Publication Data
A catalogue record for this book is
available from the British Library

ISBN 1 85223 967 0

All maps by Sharon Perks

Cover photograph by John Gillham

Typeset by Carreg Limited, Ross-on-Wye, Herefordshire

Printed by J W Arrowsmith Limited, Bristol

THE CONTRIBUTORS

Molly Askew

John C. Barrows

John Bennington

Charles Emett

Glen Hood

Pat McClelland

Jenny Preston

Margaret Ryder

Paul Sherwood

Maurice Turner

R. G. Wigham

CONTENTS

North-East

North-West

32. Clapham 6$\frac{1}{2}$m (10.5km)
33. Hardraw Force 7m (11km)
34. … and shorter version 4m (6.5km)
35. Ascent of Great Coum 7$\frac{1}{2}$m (11.5km)
36. Thwaite, Muker and Keld 7$\frac{1}{2}$m (11.5km)
37. Buckden Pike 7$\frac{1}{2}$m (11.5km)
38. Bainbridge 7$\frac{1}{2}$m (11.5km)
39. Askrigg and Worton 8m (13km)
40. Green Scar Top 8$\frac{1}{2}$m (13.5km)
41. Addlebrough Circuit 9m (14km)
42. Askrigg and Carperby 9m (14.5km)
43. Melbecks & Brownsey Moors 9m (14.5km)
44. Bainbridge and Semerwater 9m (14.5km)
45. Dent 9m (14.5km)
46. Keld Circular 10m (16km)
47. Thornton Rust Moor 10$\frac{1}{2}$m (17km)
48. Swinner Gill Gorge 11m (17.5km)
49. Gunnerside 11m (18km)
50. Castle Bolton 11m (18km)
51. Hawes and Ten End 13m (20km)
52. Hawes and Cotterdale 14m (22.5km)

South-West

53. Ilkley 3m (5km)
54. Stainforth Bridge 3m (5km)
55. Tarn Moor Circular 3$\frac{1}{2}$m (5.5km)
56. Embsay Crag 3$\frac{1}{2}$m (5.5km)
57. Haworth 4m (6.5km)
58. Numberstones End 5m (8km)
59. Bradfield 5m (8km)
60. Rivelin Valley 5m (8km)
61. … and longer version 9m (14.5km)
62. From Whirlow Park to the Ox Stones 5m (8km)
63. The Blacka Moor Circuit 5$\frac{1}{2}$m (9km)
64. Ladybower Reservoir 5$\frac{1}{2}$m (9km)
65. Norber Erratics 6m (9.5km)
66. Upper Holme Valley 6m (9.5km)
67. Duke of Devonshire's Lead Mines 6m (10km)

68. Shipley Glen and 5 Rise Locks 6m (10km)
69. Harden and St Ives 6m (10km)
70. Mickleden 7m (12km)
71. Ilkley Moor 7m (12km)
72. Todmorden 7m (12km)
73. Six Old Halls around Totley 8m (13km)
74. Settle to Malham Tarn 8m (13km)
75. Through the Cordwell Valley 8m (13km)
76. Carl Wark and Nether Padley 8m (13km)
77. Wharfedale 8m (13km)
78. High Road to Fox House $9^1/_2$m (15km)
79. Sheffield's Green Belt 10m (16km)
80. Embsay Moor 10m (16km)
81. Elgar Way Circular 13m (21km)

South-East

82. Harrogate 3m (5km)
83. Hampsthwaite and Clint 4m (6.5km)
84. Knox Manor and Smelthouses $4^1/_2$m (7km)
85. The Chevin Forest Park 5m (8km)
86. Upper Washburn Valley 5m (8km)
87. Dacre Banks 5m (8km)
88. Burton Leonard to Brearton $5^1/_2$m (9km)
89. Linton $5^1/_2$m (9km)
90. Hooton Pagnell 6m (10km)
91. Burton Leonard to Bishop Monkton 6m (10km)
92. Blubberhouses 7m (12km)
93. Shaw Mills to Ripley 7m (12km)
94. Ripley to Cayton Ghyll $7^1/_2$m (13km)
95. Shaw Mills to Brimham Rocks 8m (13km)
96. Aberford 9m (14.5km)
97. Aberford and Garforth $9^1/_4$m (14.8km)
98. Micklefield Circular $10^1/_4$m (16.4km)
99. Bramham and Aberford $10^1/_2$m (16.8km)
100. Pateley Bridge to Ramsgill $11^1/_2$m (20km)

PUBLISHER'S NOTE

We very much hope that you enjoy the routes presented in this book, which has been compiled with the aim of allowing you to explore the area in the best possible way - on foot.

We strongly recommend that you take the relevant map for the area, and for this reason we list the appropriate Ordnance Survey maps for each route. Whilst the details and descriptions given for each walk were accurate at time of writing, the countryside is constantly changing, and a map will be essential if, for any reason, you are unable to follow the given route. It is good practice to carry a map and use it so that you are always aware of your exact location.

We cannot be held responsible if some of the details in the route descriptions are found to be inaccurate, but should be grateful if walkers would advise us of any major alterations. Please note that whenever you are walking in the countryside you are on somebody else's land, and we must stress that you should *always* keep to established rights of way, and *never* cross fences, hedges or other boundaries unless there is a clear crossing point.

Remember the country code:

Enjoy the country and respect its life and work
Guard against all risk of fire
Fasten all gates
Keep dogs under close control
Keep to public footpaths across all farmland
Use gates and stiles to cross field boundaries
Leave all livestock, machinery and crops alone
Take your litter home
Help to keep all water clean
Protect wildlife, plants and trees
Make no unnecessary noise

The walks are listed by length - from approximately 1 to 12 miles - but the amount of time taken will depend on the fitness of the walkers and the time spent exploring any points of interest along the way. Nearly all the walks are circular and most offer recommendations for refreshments.

Good walking.

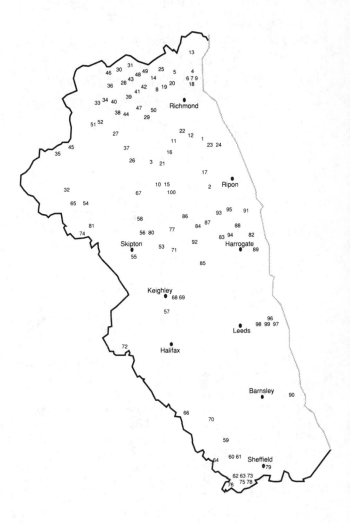

13

46 30 31
36 28 43 48 49 25 5 4
    41 42 14 8 19 20 6 7 9
33 34 40 39   18
38 44   47 50
51 52   29
27

35 45

32

65 54

81

74

Skipton
•
55

Richmond
•

22 12 1
11   23 24
16
26 3 21
17
10 15   2 Ripon
67 100   •

58   86   93 95 91
56 80 77   84 87   88
53 71 92   83 94 82
                Harrogate
                •   89
85

Keighley
• 68 69

57

Halifax
•

72

66

70

59

64 60 61 Sheffield
        •79
    62 63 73
76 75 78

Leeds
• 98 99 97
      96

Barnsley
•   90

Walk 1   MASHAM RIVERSIDE CIRCULAR   3m (5km)

Maps: OS Sheets Landranger 99; Pathfinder SE 07/17, 08/18, 27/37 and 28/38.

An easy, flat, riverside walk. N.B. The walk crosses a golf course on which no dogs are allowed.

Start: At 806227, the Market Square, Masham.

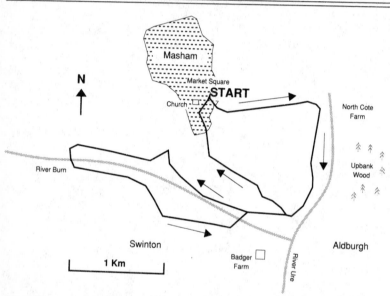

From the Market Square in **Masham**, go through the churchyard at St Mary's, then through the gate behind the church and follow the path to your left. After passing through two more gates turn right and go through the iron gate to the right of the (unobtrusive!) sewage works. Follow the path along the bank of the River Ure. When the path moves away from the river and divides, take the left fork over a stile and down a slope. This pretty woodland path, edged with wild garlic in springtime, soon runs alongside the River Burn. The lucky walker may see a kingfisher. The path crosses the road to enter a meadow. Keep straight ahead here, although the river meanders to the left. The route soon rejoins the river at a stony path right at the water's edge. In exceptionally wet weather, this section of the path may be under water, in which case it is best to return to the bridge to join the homeward stage of the walk.

When you reach the road turn left over a second bridge. Go left again through a gate on to the golf course and follow the path along the river bank to the road. Turn left over the bridge and right to retrace part of your original route. After crossing the stile into a field, turn sharp left and take the well-defined path along the field's edge. After approximately 600 yards the route goes through a large metal gate on your left. Go right through a kissing gate, back to the churchyard, and return to the start.

POINTS OF INTEREST:

Masham – The huge market place, edged by some beautiful buildings, makes Masham a very imposing town. In the 12th century it was allowed its own 'Peculier Court', a term which lives on in the name of the famous local brew – 'Old Peculier'. Theakston's has a visitors' centre, and tours of the brewery are available by appointment (tel no: 0765 89057). The Parish Church of St Mary is mentioned in the Domesday Book and the base of a 9th century cross shows there was already a church on the site in Saxon times.

REFRESHMENTS:

Bordar House Teas, Masham (tel no: 0765 89118).
The Kings Head Inn, Masham (tel no: 0765 89295).
The White Boar, Masham (tel no: 0765 89319).

Walk 2   FOUNTAINS AND STUDLEY ROYAL   3m (5km)

Maps: OS Sheets Landranger 99; Pathfinder SE 26/36 & 27/37.
This easy walk skirts the Fountains Abbey estate and passes through an 18th century landscape garden.
Start: At 270682, the car park at Fountains Abbey.

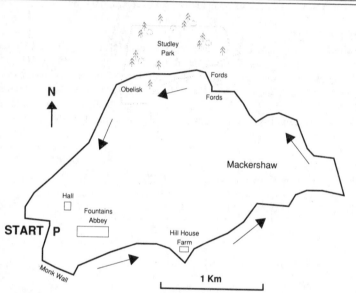

Leave the car park and turn right up the hill, bearing left as the road forks. After approximately 300 yards take the footpath on the left. As the path rises, the view of **Fountains Abbey** is particularly fine. After a mile the path goes through a gate into a field. After 100 yards the path bends to the right, goes through another gate and then after a further 50 yards bends left towards Hill House Farm. Turn left through a gate into the farm and immediately bend right in front of the barns. Follow the markers left and then right and through a gate. Take the track ahead for about 150 yards, but where it bends right go straight on, making for a gate into the woods ahead. Follow the woodland path for about ¹/₂ mile, emerging into a clearing and take the lower of the two tracks on the left, signposted to Ripon. After 200 yards turn left at the stream and cross the bridge. Turn left and after a further 200 yards go through the gate into **Studley Park**.

This is a deer park, so dogs must be kept on leads. Follow the path, which crosses the River Skell six times. After the sixth bridge (over the weir) head uphill towards the church and obelisk. Take the path in front of the church to the left, and leave the park at the gate. Follow the road to a junction, then turn left along the main road as far as the gatehouse (now a gift shop). Go straight ahead if you wish to visit Fountains Abbey, otherwise turn right for the car park.

POINTS OF INTEREST:

Fountains Abbey – (National Trust) was built in the 12th century by Benedictine monks who had adopted the Cistercian rule. The extensive ruins are in a beautiful riverside setting and are so well preserved it is easy to imagine how the abbey once looked.

Studley Park – Created between 1716 and 1781. A formal water garden, deer park and various follies are incorporated into the natural landscape.

REFRESHMENTS:

National Trust tearooms at Fountains Abbey and Studley Park.

Walk 3   SCAR RESERVOIR   4m (6.5km)

Maps: OS Sheets Landranger 98 & 99; Outdoor Leisure 30.
Easy walking, but strong footwear recommended.
Start: At 069776, the Scar Reservoir car park.

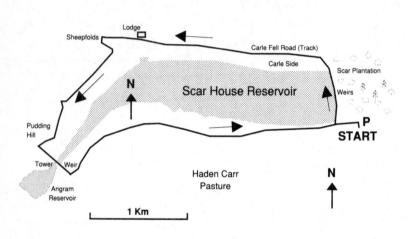

From the car park walk past the stone cottages, now used as storage places, to the dam. Note the modern memorial to the navvies here. The plaque to commemorate the official opening of the reservoir is at the beginning of the dam. Walk across to the opposite shore. You may see swifts round the towers and oyster catchers closer to the water. Turn left on the rough track and follow it up the reservoir. A steep track goes diagonally up to the right to a viewpoint at the old quarry – a rewarding diversion for the more adventurous. At a copse of trees are the ruins of the hamlet of Stone. Just beyond the trees there is a T-junction where a packhorse track comes down from Coverdale. Turn left, go through the gate and follow the path across the field to reach the top dam.

Go across the dam. To the right is the smaller Y-shaped reservoir of Angram where there is a colony of Canada geese. Beyond rises the peak of Great Whernside. At the far side of the dam go past a stone shelter with gates to keep the sheep out. Turn left and return by the waterworks road by Scar Reservoir to the car park. In the frequent damp patches bog cotton flowers. Lapwings and curlews are often heard, and in warm weather there can be adders about. Just before the car park, a track is seen winding over the hill to the right. This is a continuation of the packhorse track, which goes to **Middlesmoor**.

POINTS OF INTEREST:
Middlesmoor – The village prominent on the hilltop above Lofthouse. From its churchyard is one of the finest views in Nidderdale.

REFRESHMENTS:
The Crown Hotel, Lofthouse (tel no: 0423 75206).
The Howstean Gorge Restaurant, Lofthouse (tel no: 0423 75666). Home-made food. Children and pets welcome.

Walk 4   RICHMOND AND HUDSWELL   5m (8km)

Maps: OS Sheets Landranger 92; Pathfinder NZ 00/10.

An easy, riverside, woodland walk with just one steep climb.
Start: Market Place, Richmond.

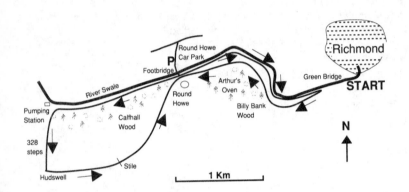

From Richmond Market Place go along New Road for a few yards into The Bar, a narrow lane. Continue down cobbled Cornforth Hill and Bridge Street to cross the River Swale on Green Bridge. Turn right between the bridge and a corner cottage into **Billy Bank Wood**. Take the broad riverside path up stream, ignoring a right track after 150 yards. Keep to the main path, climb some steps and continue up a stony, woodland path. Branch right along a level path leading to a plank bridge crossing a beck close to a 'Hudswell Woods' sign. Keeping to the main path descend through lovely woodland to cross a stile near a 'National Trust' sign and turn left along a riverside meadow. The partly hidden cave you pass on your left is called Arthur's Oven.

Beyond the meadow, cross a waymarked stile and go half-right to join a riverside path from where a wooded conical hill, Round Howe, is seen. Pass the metal footbridge spanning the Swale on your right and continue for 1 mile along the river bank into

Calfhall Wood to where your path goes half-left, away from the river, to leave the wood at a Public Footpath sign near a pumping station. Turn left and climb **328 Steps**, at the top of which there is a choice of routes. Either turn left along the top of Calfhall Wood or climb a few more steps, cross a stile and go up the path into Hudswell, a hilltop village, with a friendly pub, The George and Dragon. Turn left through the village where, just beyond the old school, there is a footpath sign fixed to a wall between Random House and Norley. Turn left here, down a lane, to cross a field, then a stile near a gate. Bear left alongside a fence to join the path that has come directly from the step's top, turning right along it to cross a watercourse. Go over a stile. Where the path ends climb wooden steps, cross a stile and go left along the edge of a field to another stile leading back into the wood. Continue along the top of the wood, ignoring the stile on your right, and leave it using a stile. Continue along a rutted track, downhill, past a 'Public Footpath' fixed to an ancient oak, to return to the metal footbridge over the Swale. Go right, briefly, and turn left over a waymarked stile near a gate and continue along the riverside. At the far end of the meadow cross a stile on to an enclosed path under Billy Bank Wood, using limestone slabs to rejoin the outward route of this excellent walk. Retrace your steps out of the wood and back to the start of the walk in Richmond Market Place.

POINTS OF INTEREST:

Billy Bank Wood – The limestone slabs here were once used as a cart-track for horses and carts from Billy Bank copper mine.

328 Steps – These were made by German prisoners during World War II to link the pumping station to the treatment plant above.

REFRESHMENTS:

The George and Dragon, Hudswell (tel no: 0748 3082). Good meals are available and children are welcome.

There are a lot of hotels, pubs and cafés in Richmond.

Maps: OS Sheets Landranger 92 & 98; Outdoor Leisure 30.
Moor, field and riverside paths, with an easy climb to Calver Hill.
Start: At 038993, the centre of Reeth.

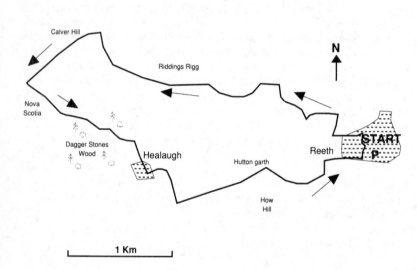

Leave Reeth by the Gunnerside road. As the buildings of Reeth are left behind a narrow enclosed lane signposted 'Skellgate' will be seen on the right. Turn up this lane, which runs between stone walls over the Riddings Farm road, to reach open moor via a wooden gate. The track accompanies a stone wall on the left and heads off across the moor. When the stone wall turns down to Riddings Farm, continue straight on over the moor until eventually the wall comes back to rejoin the track. Shortly after the wall is rejoined look for a green track heading up the moor on the right. Follow this as it climbs gradually up to Calver Hill: a broken down stone wall points the way to the summit of the hill. Leave the summit heading westward and when a crumbling wall appears on your left head towards it. Pass the wall, heading directly down the moor, keeping a corrugated tin hut on your left. On reaching a clear path cross straight over to another clear path and turn left to follow it down to the pretty village of Healaugh. Walk straight through the village to reach the main road running along Swaledale. Turn left.

As you reach the end of the village a green appears on the right. Here a signposted path to Reeth and Grinton runs from the barn corner. Follow the path through a metal gate into a meadow and alongside the left-hand wall to the river. Turn left at the river and follow the path to a suspension bridge. Do not cross the bridge, but go through a gate in the stone wall and follow the path as it heads away from the river. Cross a wooden footbridge turning right and, almost immediately, turn left at a signpost and pass through a wooden gate into an enclosed lane. Follow the lane as it moves towards the outskirts of Reeth. After a right-angled turn right ignore the first public footpath sign on your left and continue along the lane until it starts to descend. A lane on your left, with a sign for Hilary House on the corner, is where you leave the lane. Turn left at this point and follow the lane into Reeth.

REFRESHMENTS:
There is an abundance of tea rooms and pubs in Reeth, though there are none on the route.

Walks 6 and 7   A RICHMOND CIRCULAR   5m (8km) or 7m (11km)

Maps: OS Sheets Landranger 92; Pathfinder NZ 00/10.

An easy walk with riverside, waterfalls and ancient monuments.

Start: At 168007, the car park on the Green, below Culloden Tower, Richmond Bridge.

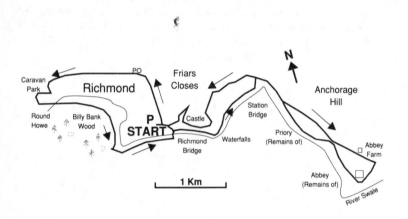

Leave the car park and follow the road across the Green to **Richmond Bridge**. Turn left before crossing the bridge and follow the road skirting the river to the impressive waterfalls below the castle. Please note, the Swale is one of the fastest flowing British rivers and can flood rapidly, take notice of all warning signs.

Continue following the riverside footpaths until you reach Station Bridge. Pass under this and follow the path almost on the water's edge for 100 yards until you have to turn left. Follow a short lane until it turns right with a footpath sign pointing to Easby Abbey. It's about ¾ mile to the remains of this Premonstratensian (a branch of the Cistercian order) House which is open to the public.

After a couple of hundred yards the path splits, take the left-hand one and follow

24

it to the Abbey: your return route can be on the other path which is closer to the river bank. Both paths are distinct.

On returning to the short lane end near Station Bridge, don't turn left but continue straight on to join the Catterick Garrison road just below St Mary's Church, follow the road uphill and left into the Market Square with its ample shops, cafés and inns as well as Holy Trinity Church and the Green Howards Museum.

Ahead of you, at the side of Barclays Bank, is a narrow road. Take this and follow the upper path when the road goes down to the waterfalls. You reach the Castle Walk which takes you around the outside of the Norman castle with very fine views down to the river. This in turn rejoins the Market Square at the top of New Road.

We are now at an ideal starting point for a longer walk, touring the town regarded as one of the most visually enjoyable small towns in England. Apart from the Castle, the Green Howards Museum, The Greyfriars Tower (Franciscan) and the Georgian Theatre there is much to see.

To quickly return to the car park, go down New Road to Bargate and back to the Green. Our walk continues from the bottom of Bargate and crosses Richmond Bridge. Turn right through a wide gate and follow the track for 100 yards, to where a low level path at the water's edge continues for almost $1/4$ mile to the bend in the river. From here the paths re-unite and continue well-defined to Round Howe. Although it is not shown on the 1:25,000 map (though it is shown on the 1:50,000) there is a footbridge crossing the Swale to the Round Howe car park. Follow the footpath through the caravan site and on to Reeth Road, passing the Convent on your right. At the top of Reeth Road you will see an interesting yellow plaque on the wall of a building on your left: it marks the line of totality of the 1927 solar eclipse. From here continue straight ahead downhill to the car park.

POINTS OF INTEREST:

Richmond – Well known for its 'Sweet Lass of Richmond Hill', Richmond is the gateway to Swaledale, the most northern, true Yorkshire Dale. Although it can become very crowded in the tourist season it is in general quite an easy place to park. The bridge was built in 1789. The Culloden Tower was built in 1746 (as a monument to the Jacobite defeat). Tourist Information Office (tel no: 0748 5994).

REFRESHMENTS:

Numerous cafés and inns in the town.

25

Walk 8   MARSKE TO SKELTON MOOR   5¹/₂ m (9km)

Maps: OS Sheets Landranger 92; Outdoor Leisure 30.
Mainly on well-drained farm tracks.
Start: At 105006, near the Post Office in Marske.

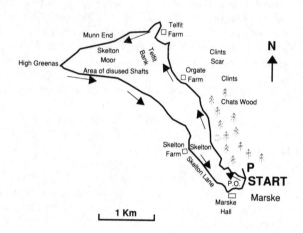

From the Post Office walk along the small row of houses which incorporates the old school whose sundial is engraved *Tempus Fugit*. Go through a gate with a yellow waymark, heading for Clints. The track crosses a cattle grid and passes the Marske Methodist Church as it heads down into beautiful old woodland. You can smell wild garlic in places. As you come out of the woodland area, there is a fork in the track. Take the left fork, continuing through the woods and then between two fences up on to open ground. Continue to Orgate Farm where the concrete track splits into two – one going into the farm and the other down to Orgate Bridge. Take neither of them(!), but follow a grassy pathway between the two keeping downhill of the farm. Once past the farm, go up through a gate and keep the field walls on your left until they end. At this point, do not go uphill, but follow various small paths until you are down by the Marske Beck at a recently restored pack bridge, a beautiful spot.

26

Cross the pack bridge and turn left through a gate. Go right to walk through the farmer's field. Grass is a crop to the farmer so walk in single file up to the track where you turn right. Follow the track uphill, past Telfit Farm, through fields until you are out on the open moorland of Skelton Moor. Follow the track across the moor to the corner of the field at a gate, where you will find an old stone gatepost lying down (it makes a grand seat!). Do not go through the gate but instead turn left, heading east again along the fence and looking towards Hutton's Monument, the obelisk on the skyline. Follow the boundary path. It is joined on the left by another track and then goes through a gate. Be prepared, as you come over the rise, for a spectacular view of Clints Scar and the valley in which you walked earlier. Follow the track down to a road where you turn right and walk down past Skelton Farm with wild aniseed growing in the hedges. At the end of the road turn left into **Marske**, go over the bridge and up the hill to the Post Office.

POINTS OF INTEREST:
Markse – A beautiful village with sundials on several houses. At the bridge, there is a tiny gap in the wall and steps leading down the Beck.

REFRESHMENTS:
The nearest refreshments are in Richmond, where you will find many pubs and ice-cream shops.

Walk 9   RICHMOND BEACON   6m (9.5km)

Maps: OS Sheets Landranger 92; Pathfinder NZ 00/10.

An upland walk with fine views.

Start: Nuns Close car park, Richmond.

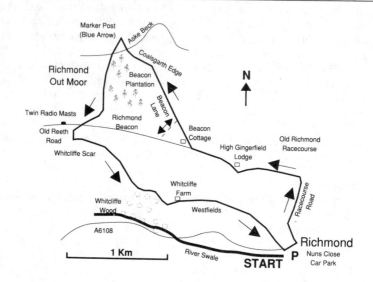

From the car park go left up Hurgill Road and right into Quarry Road, climbing steeply. At a road junction continue straight ahead along Racecourse Road and where the road bends left go straight ahead along a signposted path and over a wall stile into Old Richmond Racecourse. Turn left, passing the old stone Race Judge's Box. Beyond this go through a white gate to the Old Reeth Road. Turn right along the road, past High Gingerfield Lodge, and after $^1/_2$ mile turn right just before Beacon Cottage into unsigned Beacon Lane and continue for 2 miles along Coalsgarth Edge. On the way, to your left, **Richmond Beacon** on Beacon Hill is seen. A short detour of about $^3/_4$ mile along Beacon Lane, on a public right of way, to the Beacon is worth taking. Having seen the beacon from close quarters, return to Beacon Lane and continue, along it north-west to Aske Beck. Cross on stepping stones and immediately go through the facing wooden gate, beyond which climb along the track for $^1/_4$ mile to a metal gate displaying blue waymarkers. Do not go through this gate. Instead, follow the path on its left to a white post marked with blue arrows, where you turn left along a path southwards over Richmond Out Moor with Beacon Plantation on your left and twin radio masts ahead on the horizon. Re-cross Aske Beck to reach, two tall waymarker posts which direct you over the moor to exit through a gate to the Old Reach Road. Turn right along it for 50yds to where a public footpath sign points you over a ladder stile in a wall. Now go half-right for a little way along a path which merges with a tractor track before going south across rough pasture, aiming for the top of a monument seen peeping over a wall. Go through a small gate to the two remaining of three memorial stones set 24ft apart, marking Willance's Leap. You are now on **Whitcliffe Scar**, from where there are panoramic views of Swaledale, distant Pen Hill in Wensleydale and Great Whernside. Go left along Whitcliffe Wood. Bear left at some gorse bushes to exit through an open gateway in a facing fence. Continue along a track which soon curves right down the hillside to a gated farm road opposite High Leases Farm. Turn left along it, passing Whitcliff Farm on your left and follow the surfaced road down Westfields for a mile to Richmond and the end of a good walk.

POINTS OF INTEREST:

Richmond Beacon – An old signal station standing 1045ft above sea level. It was lit when the Spanish Armada passed by.

Whitcliffe Scar – One day in 1606, while hunting in bad weather, Robert Willance survived when the horse he was riding took three spectacular leaps across ground that was falling away before it. Each of the leaps was at least 24ft long and on the third one horse and rider plunged 200ft over Whitcliffe Scar. Willance erected three memorial stones on the spot, of which two remain.

REFRESHMENTS:

There are plenty of hotels, pubs and cafés in Richmond but none *en route*.

Walk 10   NIDDERDALE AND RAMSGILL   6m (10km)

Maps: OS Sheets Landranger 99; Pathfinder SE 07/17.

Easy, with a short steep lane out of Lofthouse.

Start: At 119710, in the Lofthouse road, Ramsgill.

Continue along the Lofthouse road, over the packhorse bridge, then turn right on the lane signposted Bouthwaite. Go up the lane, noting the old station house on the right, – a relic of the Nidderdale Light Railway. At Bouthwaite, turn left on the footpath past Grange Farm, once owned by Fountains Abbey. Follow the path on the field track past the lower edge of a conifer plantation, then past the back of a farm and down to the road. Cross the stiles at either side of the road. Follow the old railway track, then go to the right across a field and through a beggar's stile to the road. The old vicarage is on the hill in front of you. Cross the road diagonally to the left, go over a stile and follow the path which brings you out at the back of the Crown Hotel, **Lofthouse**. Turn left through the village. At the main road turn right, signposted Middlesmoor, then, almost immediately, turn left over the little bridge across Howstean Beck.

If you wish to extend your walk, turn right and walk up the lane for $1/2$ mile to the entrance to Howstean Gorge. There is a café here, and toilets. The walk down the gorge (entrance fee) brings you out at a wicket gate just above the little bridge.

Left as you stand on the bridge, there is a rough lane which takes you past the caravan site, steeply uphill to cottages. Take the next turn left, along a walled lane to a bridge. Just above are ruined buildings and a channel has been cut in the stream bed.

Continue forward by field paths past Low West House. The path gradually descends and you return to Ramsgill through a farm yard.

POINTS OF INTEREST:

The walk follows part of the Nidderdale Way, a long distance footpath. In April the dale is at its best, with fresh greens and many lambs.

Lofthouse – In the centre of the village is a fountain, the War Memorial. Further up the road is a horse trough, commemorating the Armistice.

REFRESHMENTS:

The Crown Hotel, Lofthouse (tel no: 0423 75206).
The Yorke Arms, Ramsgill (tel no: 0423 75243).

Walk 11   COVERHAM ABBEY   6m (10km)

Maps: OS Sheets Landranger 99; Outdoor Leisure 30.
An easy walk, with many points of interest. Some paths have been diverted, and are not as shown by the Ordnance Survey.
Start: At 127877, Middleham market place.

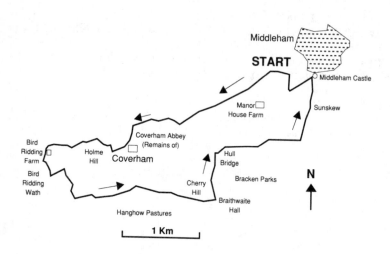

From the Richard III hotel, pass through the arch alongside and up the yard beyond, turning right at the top. Turn left along the east side of the castle, then right at the stile by the bungalow. Go straight across the field and through the gate in the left-hand fence, climbing the steep mound of the original **Middleham Castle** to reach the best viewpoint for appreciating the massive size of the present one. On leaving the mound, follow the left-hand fence northwards towards the road, but turn left over the stile just before reaching it. The path follows the road keeping you away from the traffic for a while, but at a small clump of trees cross a stile, right, to emerge on to the common. Turn left over another stile and follow the field boundary on the left, parallel to the road. About 1 mile from Middleham, and just past the pool, turn left through the gate at a footpath signpost and turn right, parallel to the road but behind the hedge. Cross two stiles, go through a hedge gap and two gates, to emerge on the road at the entrance to Coverham Abbey Farm.

Turn left down the farm drive and right at the crossways at the bottom, by the abbey ruins. Part of the abbey church is still standing in the garden of Garth Cottage and many fragments are built into nearby houses. Continue along the track, under the arch of the former abbey gatehouse, turning right through a wicket gate just before the house and climbing past a small waterfall into the churchyard. Although the church is redundant, memorials testify to the great size of this once-important parish. Leave the churchyard by the north gate, turning left along the main road towards Carlton. Follow it for 200 yards before turning left, across a stream and a stile. Go right, following the stream side to emerge on a farm drive. Turn left here, then left again in a few yards by the cottage, to descend an overgrown track to the footbridge at Bird Ridding Wath. Cross the bridge and follow the hedged path up to the road, where you turn left. Go right through the first gate and follow the left-hand fence up to its continuation by a line of old beeches, leading to a cross wall. The view is even better from higher up, so turn right for 40 yards, cross the stile and climb straight up the field beyond to cross the wooden fence at the top. Turn left and follow the field edge through a gate and over a stile, turning right through the next gate, then left to follow the field boundary down to a wicket gate into Hanghow Lane. Turn right along the lane for 3/4 mile, then left down the bridleway opposite **Braithwaite Hall**. Go straight ahead after the second gate, then swing right down to the bridge. After crossing the River Cover, turn right to pick up a clear track which climbs the bank and continue in the same line across the field above. Pass through the hedge and turn left to the gate by the barn. Turn half right and head for the middle of three barns visible ahead, but turn left at the fence to pass the left-hand barn. Go through the gate and turn left for Middleham.

POINTS OF INTEREST:

Middleham Castle – Is open to the public at the usual times.

Braithwaite Hall – A National Trust property that can be visited on request.

Walk 12 JERVAULX ABBEY AND THORNTON STEWARD $7^1/_2$m (12km)

Maps: OS Sheets Landranger 99; Pathfinder SE 08/18.

An easy, low level walk through pleasant parkland, along quiet country lanes and delightful riverside paths.

Start: Jervaulx Abbey car park.

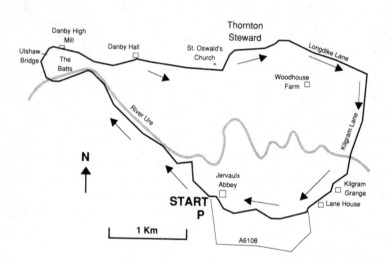

From the car park go left along the A6108 for almost $^1/_2$ mile and, just past the bridge over Lee Gill Beck, turn right through a gate marked 'Private Property – Footpath Only – Dogs On Lead Please' and waymarked with a yellow arrow. Go along the path ahead and through another gate and, at the confluence of Lee Gill beck and the River Ure, turn left, upstream. Stay close to the river, on your right, for 2 miles, the final part being along the River Cover, to reach Cover Bridge. The white robed monks of Jervaulx frequently used this popular path, from which can be seen a great variety of birdlife, including herons and swans. Turn right over Cover bridge, hump-backed and built in 1766, and continue past *olde worlde* Cover Bridge Inn. Go right at a road junction and cross the River Ure using Ulshaw Bridge. Beyond, go right passing, on your left, the

Catholic church of St Simon and St Jude. Keep going forward for almost $^1/_2$ mile and where the road swings left, continue straight ahead along an unsurfaced track. The disused water-driven corn mill you pass on leaving the surfaced road is Danby High Mill: the one seen from the unsurfaced road, near a tidy cottage, is Danby Low Mill.

Enter Danby Low Park through a gate and continue through the parkland using a carriageway which soon turns towards Danby Hall, the splendid Elizabethan home of the Scrope family. Turn right on approaching the hall gates, passing an ancient oak, and make for a metal gate ahead, not the wooden one on your right. Continue eastwards, keeping close to the lower edge of a field and exit through a white gate in a fence. The way ahead is marked by blue arrows. Follow these, crossing four fields to reach isolated St Oswald's church. This little church, with its medieval bellcote and two bells, is the oldest in Wensleydale. Continue along the road for $^1/_2$ mile to the village of Thornton Steward from where, because it is set a little above the surrounding countryside, the views of lower Wensleydale are extensive. Leave the village at its eastern end and go along Longdike Lane. After 1 mile, at a cross roads, turn right, along Kilgram Lane for $^1/_2$ mile to recross the River Ure on a bridge that is said to have been built by the Devil in one night. Continue along Kilgram Lane for a further $^1/_2$ mile, passing Kilgram Grange, and where it curves left continue straight ahead to enter Jervaulx Park. The way ahead is clear, the parkland magnificent and soon the walk climaxes when the theocratic remains of Jervaulx Abbey, silent and haunting, meet the eye. The car park is very close now but tarry a while, for the Abbey merits more than a passing glance.

POINTS OF INTEREST:
That part of the River Ure where the Cover flows into it is guarded by a Kelpie.
A sundial, dated 1674, is fixed to Ulshaw Bridge.
Should you reach Jervaulx Abbey as daylight drains from the sky and should an icy chill envelope you despite the heat generated by your walk, don't hang around. You never know!

REFRESHMENTS:
Jervaulx Abbey Gardens café and tea garden. Open April to October.
The Jervaulx Hall Hotel, (tel no: 0677 60235).
The Crown Bridge Inn, (tel no: 0969 23250).

Walk 13   GILLING WEST AND RAVENSWORTH   8m (13km)

Maps: OS Sheets Landranger 92; Pathfinder SE 00/10.

A pleasant, fairly easy walk with one steep climb.

Start: Gilling West village.

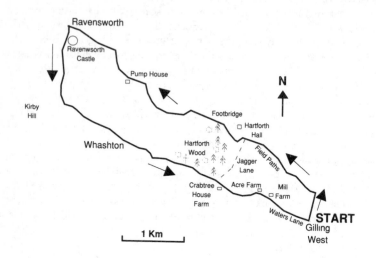

Leave the village at the north end of Gilling Bridge, going left at a Public Footpath sign and through a gap in the wall ahead. Pass Town End Farm and go west through fields on a clear route for 1 mile to Hartforth. Turn left at farm buildings and take a broad track, **Jagger Lane**, over Hartforth Beck using an ornate bridge. Go right through a white gate and take a path across a field with Hartforth Hall and ruined church seen on your right. Cross a metal footbridge and turn left, upstream, edging a field. At a gap near a rusty gate turn left along a track to the old Hartforth Saw Mill. Follow the yellow markers left, round the mill, and cross a plank bridge to a stile near a gate. Turn right, upstream, through delightful stiled and gated meadows to Comfort Lane, just south of Whashton Bridge. Cross (the lane, not the bridge) and continue upstream close to Holm Beck where herons are often seen on your right. Soon after passing a small brick pump house, and where the beck comes down from the right, go straight ahead across a field along a right of way but with an undefined route, aiming for a stile where the hedge ahead ends. Continue ahead over two stiles, aiming for the top inset right corner of the meadow. Cross a stile near a gate on your right, partly hidden by hawthorn bushes, and go forward to another stile just past some holly and hawthorn bushes. Turn left over a stone stile and go diagonally right over the next two stiled pastures, with good views of ruined **Ravensworth Castle** ahead, to reach a road. Turn right for $^1/_2$ mile to enter delightful Ravensworth village. Go through it as far as the Bay House Inn. The mansion opposite belongs to Ian Botham. Turn left, passing the Primary School, and where the road bends right go straight ahead through a handgate near a gate marked 'Larklands'. Continue up a track for a short distance to a stile on your left, tucked in between two ash trees. Go over the stile, then right, diagonally, up rough pasture, heading for a stile where a wall meets a hawthorn hedge. Go up the side of two fields and climb steeply on to Kirby Hill, which is well worth exploring. Leave this little hilltop village along the road past the church on your right and the Shoulder of Mutton on your left. After $^1/_2$ mile go straight over a crossroads to reach, after another $^1/_4$ mile, Whashton village. At the bottom of the village bear right along a lane marked 'No Through Road'. Go downhill for $^1/_4$ mile and immediately after crossing a white railed cattle grid, turn left along a field and out through a gate. Follow the uphill path, between trees, with Hartforth Wood on your left. Cross Leadmill Gill Beck on stepping stones and continue eastwards along Leadmill Lane to Jagger Lane. Go left along it for a few yards, then right along a clear farm road past Crabtree House Farm into Waters Lane and so back to Gilling West.

POINTS OF INTEREST:

Jagger Lane – An old pack horse trail. It was once an important route for carrying salt, lead and coal between Durham and Wensleydale.
Ravensworth Castle – Built in the 12th century, was once the stronghold home of the Fitzhugh family.

REFRESHMENTS:

The Angel Hotel, Gilling West (tel no: 0748 3811).
The White Swan Inn, Gilling West (tel no: 0748 2778).
The Bay Horse, Ravensworth (tel no: 0325 718328).
The Shoulder of Mutton, Kirby Hill (tel no: 0748 2772). This is an excellent mid-way refreshment stop. Walkers are made very welcome here.

Walk 14   REETH AND LANGTHWAITE   8m (13km)

Maps: OS Sheets Landranger 92 & 98; Outdoor Leisure 30.

A grand walk in Herriot country. Superb views.

Start: Reeth.

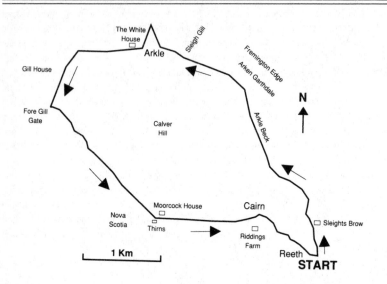

From Reeth take the Langthwaite road for $^{1}/_{2}$ mile to reach a stile on the right signed 'Langthwaite', just beyond a house, 'Sleights Brow'. The way ahead, over meadows, is well signposted with yellow blobs and arrows and goes along and above the west bank of Arkle Beck. In the first $^{1}/_{2}$ mile there are at least nine stiles and, wedged in a tree, a sign reading 'Langthwaite – Reeth'. When you reach a facing gate leading to a farm track, do not go downhill to the bridge over the beck. Just cross the track and follow the markers. After $^{1}/_{2}$ mile, where the path goes alongside a waymarked wall on your right, the way is particularly muddy. Continue through a small gate, cross a little beck and go past the front of West Raw Croft Farm. Go over a farm road and a field, then through a gate and on, through another gateway. Take the faint trod forking left, uphill, to an easily missed footpath signpost. Turn right here, continue along the field and exit over a stile. Where Fore Gill Beck crosses the route there is no bridge, but usually it is possible to cross dry shod. If too much water is flowing, make a short detour left until a crossing is possible. Once across this feeder go over a stile, then cross Arkle Beck on a railed footbridge and continue upstream to **Langthwaite**.

Leave it over an ancient bridge across Arkle Beck on your left, then turn left along the road to Arkle Town Hamlet. There turn right along a stony track, passing the whitewashed 'White House', on your right, to reach open moor. Follow the track, climbing steeply past Gill House on your left with the way deteriorating and becoming boggy. Head for a wooden gate and continue up trackless moor, passing Bouldershaw House outbuildings. Beyond go up a farm track to join the quiet Langthwaite – Low Row road. Turn left for $^1/_2$ mile, to where there are two road signs, 'Z-bend and 1:5'. The watersplash – Fore Gill Gate, a popular picnic site – at the bottom of the hill ahead is used in the opening of the television series 'All Creatures Great and Small'. However, the way ahead from the hilltop is left through a wooden gate signposted 'Bridleway Only – No Vehicles' and along a track on to Reeth Low Moor. Keep close to the wall on your right and, where the track turns left, bear half right along a faint track which skirts the side of Cringley Hill. Continue downhill, passing a wire fenced enclosure on your right, then going below a three walled enclosure on your left. Where the track forks, go right to a parallel track which will take you to Novia Scotia and Thirns farms and by Moorcock House back to the moor. Turn right and continue eastwards close to an intake wall on your right and, to the left ahead, the summit of Calver Hill (1599 ft). When Riddings Farm can be seen below on the right, go through a corner gate on your right and along Skelgate Lane, muddy in places, to join the B6270. Turn left down School Bank into Reeth.

POINTS OF INTEREST:
There are fine views across Arkle Beck to Fremington Edge all the way to Langthwaite. **Langthwaite** – A church built at Arkle Town hamlet in 1145 was demolished in 1818 and rebuilt in Langthwaite. The churchyard with its gravestones, tilted by time to odd angles remains.
Langthwaite's ancient bridge has been featured in several episodes of 'All Creatures Great and Small', as has its seventeenth century pub, The Red Lion Inn. It is one of Britain's most televised pubs, having been used in Walt Disney's 'Escape from the Dark', the ITV series 'Andy Robson' and a 'A Woman of Substance'.

REFRESHMENTS:
There are several pubs and cafés in Reeth.
The Red Lion, Langthwaite (tel no: 0748 84218).

Walk 15   RAMSGILL TO LOFTHOUSE   8m (13km)

Maps: OS Sheets Landranger 99; Pathfinder SE 07/17.
A pleasant walk, in part along the Nidderdale Way.
Start: Ramsgill.

From Ramsgill take the route out of the village towards Bouthwaite. In Bouthwaite turn left just past the chapel and follow the Nidderdale Way sign, going along a lane and left into a farmyard. Go through the yard and over a wooden bridge which spans Lul Beck. Over the bridge go right over a stile in the wall. Follow the wood side up to a set of wooden steps over a high wall. Turn left and follow the path along the shawl to a second set of steps. In front now is a farm house: pass to the right of this and on to a chalk stone road. At the next gate turn slightly uphill towards a plantation. Keep to the left of the plantation and go over two stiles. At the second stile turn left and go down to a road. Ignore the Nidderdale Way sign straight across and turn right along the road towards Lofthouse. After $1/2$ mile take the Nidderdale Way to the right and cross the fields to Lofthouse village (*see* Walk 10). The path reaches the road at the side of the Crown Hotel.

Turn right up the hill towards Masham and continue uphill on the road for about 1 mile. Turn right off the road past a sign 'Not Suitable for Vehicles'. Follow the track to a gate with a fire warning sign. Just after the gate the track splits: follow the right fork with a dry stone wall on the right until the track is closed in by walls on both sides. To the left can be seen the millstone grit outcrop of Jenny Twigg and daughter Tibb on the skyline. The track now begins to drop away down to a bridge over Lul Beck for the second time. After the bridge the track rises to the junction with the route from Low Ash Head Moor shooting box. Take the track to the right, which runs alongside the big plantation and continue to the junction with the track from Dallow Gill and Dalton Lodge. Turn right past another sign 'Unsuitable for Motor Vehicles' and take the very rough road down to Bouthwaite and on to Ramsgill and the start.

Please note that the pull to Lofthouse is very steep and long. In addition the moorland track is exposed and waterproof clothing is recommended.

REFRESHMENTS:
The Crown Hotel, Lofthouse (tel no: 0423 75206).

Walk 16 ARNAGILL MOOR 9m (14km)

Maps: OS Sheets Landranger 99; Pathfinder SE 07/17.

The highest point of the walk, at 356m, is high enough to give extensive views, but is reached without steep climbing.

Start: At 156787, to the north of Leighton Reservoir.

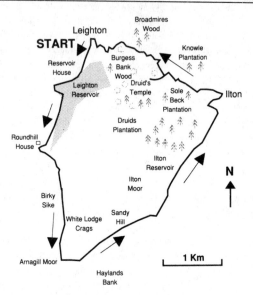

From the roadside parking area cross the bridge and follow the road towards Lofthouse for 400 yards before turning off left along the Water Board road to Roundhill Reservoir. Cross the dam and go straight ahead up the hillside, before passing through the gateway in the wall on your right. Turn left now, and make for the gate at the top of the field, turning half right after passing through it to follow a clear track across the moor. The path is roughly parallel to Arnagill, on your right, but when the way becomes less distinct near Birky Sike turn half right to pass along the top of White Lodge Crags. The path is now clear again, and consists of a slightly raised causeway which eventually emerges on to a hard track crossing Arnagill Moor. Turn left along this high-level route and follow it across the heather, with fine views to the west, for nearly 1½ miles. After crossing a small bridge fork left and follow the track downhill to the end of the moor.

After the moor gate, continue forward to a junction just short of Ilton. Turn left and follow the track to a triangular green, turning left across it to join the road at a telephone box. Turn left here, down the hill, but after 200 yards, where the road bends right, turn left through a gate, then right along the wall to cross an awkward ditch. Go straight on down the field and cross a stile into the woods. Follow a clear track down towards the stream, turning left at one point to find the stepping stones. Cross near a beautifully-constructed kiln, and follow the track uphill to a stile, crossing it and turning left immediately through a gate. Turn right uphill by a wall to High Knowle, crossing a stile to pass in front of the house, then turning right through the gate beyond the barn. This farm drive takes you out on to the road, where you turn left to find the **Druids Temple** beyond the road end.

On leaving, retrace your steps to the cattle grid and go back down the lane for 50 yards, then turn left through a gate to follow the woodland edge. Head for the massively-built gateposts – more sham monoliths – slightly to the right, turning left after passing between them and again follow the woodland edge to a track leading left to a gate. Pass through and turn right to pick up a stony track. Follow this downhill to another gate where the track ends. Turn half left across the pasture beyond, heading to the right of a little copse to reach a gate at the edge of yet more woodland. Passing through the gate, follow the twists and turns of the green track ahead, with a sharp left turn along the river bank, on its way to an old stone bridge. After crossing, the track turns left, then right up the hill before passing through a gate on the left. Turn half right now, across the meadow to a gate above the barn. Go through, and straight ahead to a gate below Leighton Hall. Turn left into the farmyard leading to the road. Turn left and follow the road back to the reservoir.

POINTS OF INTEREST:

Druids Temple – A Gothic folly built around 1820 for William Danby of Swinton Hall. It is a miniature Stonehenge some 100ft long and 50ft wide, oval in shape and with standing stones 10ft high. During a period of unemployment Danby paid local men one shilling per day to construct it.

Maps: OS Sheets Landranger 99; Pathfinder SE 27/37.

A level walk over easy country with surprisingly extensive views.

Start: At 227743, by the green off the main street at the west end of Kirkby Malzeard village.

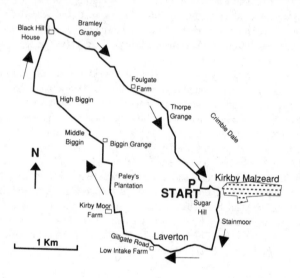

Take the Laverton road at the west end of the village street and turn left immediately into the 'back lane'. Follow this as far as the sports field, turning half right across the field so as to leave it short of the tennis courts. At the cemetery signpost turn right over the stile, instead of going straight ahead, and follow the right-hand hedge to another stile. Cross and continue ahead until, at a gate on the right, you turn half left to emerge by way of a third stile on to a lane. Turn right and follow the lane to a T-road. Go right again through Laverton village. At its western extremity, where the road turns right, go straight ahead along a bridleway. Follow the bridleway, making a sharp turn right at Low Intake farm, for nearly a mile to a fork. Turn right to Kirkby Moor. Turn left along the road, then right almost immediately (before a farm that is not as shown on the OS map) following the right-hand hedge until Paley's Plantation is reached. The footpath through it soon becomes a clear track leading to a road. Turn left, then right after 200 yards, along a bridleway serving the two Biggin farms. After 250 yards turn left, leaving Biggin Grange to your right, and continue into Middle Biggin farmyard. Turn left here, through a gate, and go forward up the field to the crest of the hill, where there should be a view back to **Kirkby Malzeard** – and perhaps far beyond.

After passing through the first gate on the hilltop you are faced by two more, in the cross-wall. Pass through the right-hand one and turn half right, across the field, to a gate visible in the far corner. On leaving it, head for the distant barn, the former site of Upper Biggin farm. Take the gate next to the ruin, then turn half right to reach a gate leading into Wreaks Lane. Turn left along this delightful lane for $^1/_4$ mile, then right after it becomes a tarred road. Follow this turn north for 1 mile to a right turning just after Black Hill House. Pass Bramley Grange to reach Foulgate Nook, where you cross the stile opposite the house and turn half left across the field to a stile in the left-hand wall. On crossing it, follow the northern hedge of a narrow field to find the next stile. Go over and follow the right-hand hedge to a barn which you go round on the north side. Cross the stile ahead and continue with the hedge on your right towards Thorpe Grange. Turn right at the copse before the farm, pass through a gate on your left, then turn half right, crossing the field to another gate. Go right through a further gate in quick succession and straight down the field to another. After this, follow the left-hand hedge to emerge on a bridleway by a stream. Turn left and cross the footbridge to reach a hedged green lane. About 150 yards after passing a building on the left, turn right over a hidden stile towards a bungalow, but turn left before it going over two stiles. Pass between wooden sheds, then turn right into a hedge corner where steps lead down into the lane at the west end of the village.

POINTS OF INTEREST:
Kirkby Malzeard – The de Mowbrays, Lords of Kirkby Malzeard, were great benefactors of monasteries, Bramley and Biggin Granges being granted to Fountains Abbey and Newburgh Priory respectively.

REFRESHMENTS:
The Henry Jenkins Inn, Kirkby Malzeard (tel no: 076583 557).

Walk 18   **RICHMOND AND GILLING**   9m (14.5km)

Maps: OS Sheets Landranger 92 & 93; Pathfinder NZ 00/10 & 20/30.

Lesser known country to the east and north of Richmond.
Start: Richmond Market Place.

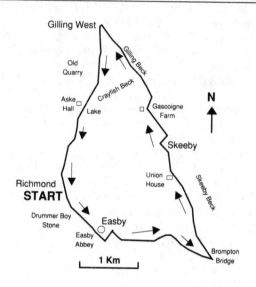

Go along the Station Road and beyond St Mary's Church turn left along a short lane, then right along Easby Low Road, signposted Easby Abbey, into Clink Bank Wood. Where the path divides below Clink Bank take either path: they rejoin later. However, the top path passes, on the left, wedged behind a gate post, an upright slab of stone called the **Drummerboy Stone**. After about 900 yards cross a waymarked stile and turn right across a field towards Easby Abbey, ahead. Cross a stile near kennels, go left by Abbey Mill and follow the road to the Abbey. Continue uphill to Easby village and turn right for 450 yards along a lane. Where it bends left go through a gate with a 'Public Bridleway' sign, turn right along a field hedge and follow yellow arrows, first crossing a fence, then turning left along it for three fields to Brompton car park. Turn right along the B6271, but just before Brompton Bridge turn left through a gap and follow the track north along Skeeby Beck. Cross a disused railway and go up the right side of the next field to where a track keeps close to a neat hedge. Go through a gate, along the track, through another gate and along the edge of a field to a gate on a corner. Continue through scrub, then a gate into pasture. Keep close to the hedge, left, to join a clearer track coming from the right. Take this track, leftwards, towards Union House Farm. Before the farm go through a gate, right, ignoring the waymarker. Bear left under power cables to some gates. Turn left, following yellow arrows, up the field's edge, turning right, then left to a waymarked fence post in a corner. Turn half-right, cross a field and exit over a stile. Cross the next field, go through a waymarked opening, bear half-right along a track, go over a stile and across another field to Skeeby. Turn right on the A6108, then left, opposite the church, into a signposted opening and follow the track for four fields. Where the track ends cross the stile ahead and continue down the hillside. Turn right along a track to pass Gascoigne Farm on your left. When the track reaches Gilling Beck do not cross, but go over a stile, left. Go upstream for a mile. Beyond the sewage works bear half-left for two fields into a play area and continue via Millgate into Gilling West. Turn left along the B6274 for $^1/_2$ mile to a footpath sign on the right. Go through the right-hand of three gates along a track going left and cross a stile on your left. Pass a barn and take the path by a wall with a quarry on the right. Cross stiles over the next two fields to exit through a gate to Aske Workshops. Turn right past **Aske Hall**. Stay on the drive and at the gateway entrance bear right along a path over Aske Park. Go through a waymarked gate, down a woodland path, cross a forest drive and a one-railed bridge. At the top of woodland cross a stile and go right along the field edge, then left up the same field. Follow yellow arrows to a kissing gate in the Richmond Golf Course fence. Follow the white marker posts to Gallowgate, then go downhill into Richmond.

POINTS OF INTEREST:

The Drummerboy Stone – Erected to mark the last spot a boy was heard as he drummed while exploring the underground passages reputed to exist between Richmond Castle and Easby Abbey.

Aske Hall – An elegant building, is the home of the Marquess of Zetland.

REFRESHMENTS:

There are many pubs, hotels and cafés in Richmond.

The Travellers' Rest, Skeeby (tel no: 0748 2030).

The Angel, Gilling West (tel no: 0748 3811).

The White Swan, Gilling West (tel no: 0748 2778).

Walks 19 and 20   **HOLGATE PASTURES**   9³/₄m (15.5km) or
6m (9.5km)
Maps: OS Sheets Landranger 92; Outdoor Leisure 30.
Varied walks with beautiful views.
Start: At 073042, the crossroads on minor road from Newsham
to Marske.

To reach the start take the road marked 'Helwith 6.5' at a T-junction in Newsham and drive for about 5 miles, passing over two cattle grids until you come to the crossroads. There is ample parking at the crossroads.

Take the road signposted to Hurst heading south-west. Do not go into Holgate Farm but continue down into the stream valley with a ford and footbridge, an excellent place for a very early lunch! Cross the stream and continue on the track between two walls. Go through a gate to where the track becomes a metalled road again. Walk through the hamlets of Washfold and Hurst, noticing the old chimneys on the left, and continue (when the metalling stops) to follow a well-defined track through the old mining remains. Lots of minerals (quartz and galena to name but two) are to be found in this area. Some excellent grouse butts will be seen but resist the temptation to stop for lunch (if you have not already done so!) for as you come over the rise towards the National Park Boundary, you will see the most glorious views over Arkengarthdale (to the north), Calver Hill (ahead) and Gibbon Hill (south). Do not go through the stone wall which marks the Boundary but turn left and walk along it on a well-trodden path for about $1^1/_4$ miles. The views are to the east now towards Marske and Helwith. You will come to a wall and, after going through the gate/opening in the wall, follow the track which heads diagonally away to the left towards Owlands Farm. There turn right and go down to the metalled road. At the road turn right and walk for about $^1/_2$ mile until you see a road on the left signposted for Greenas Farm. Take it and walk down to where it ends at three gates. Take one of the gates, turn right and head diagonally across the field on a track. On the left is a particularly spectacular view of Shaw Beck and Shaw Tongue: you should be able to pick out where you have been and be able to see your car. The track bears round to the left down the hill. Follow it down to the Shaw Beck at Helwith, where you will find a ford and footbridge. The track then becomes a metalled road which you follow back up to your car.

The longer route is described above. To shorten it to 6 miles, turn left near the telephone box in Washfold and walk down to reach the road for Greenas Farm, continuing as described from there.

POINTS OF INTEREST:

Look out for rabbits in the Holgate section. The hillsides are alive with them.
The area near Hurst was a mining area and is scattered with spoil heaps and old shafts and chimneys.
There are many wild flowers to be seen in the area near Owlands farm and in the lower parts of this walk.
You will see many curlews and lapwings on the moorland edges.

REFRESHMENTS:

The Pipes Tavern, Newsham (tel no: 0388 21223). Bar meals and snacks. Children are welcome.

DALE EDGE

Maps: OS Sheets Landranger 99; Outdoor Leisure 30.

A mainly high level walk, with two quite steep climbs, giving splendid views of Nidderdale.

Start: At 101734, the car park in Lofthouse.

From the car park walk up the main street and leave the village by the Masham road, bearing left after a few hundred yards on to a signposted bridleway. This green lane linked the former Fountains Abbey granges, but after 1 mile, at Thrope farm, you leave it by the gate below the barn, on the right, and climb steeply up the field to the gate visible at the top. Go through and turn left along the fence to another gate. After this you take the steep right turn up the hillside by the fence (not as shown on OS map). By Thrope Plantation the path bends sharply left, continuing to climb to the moor-wall gate. The best of the views appear on passing through the gate and climbing a rocky slope straight ahead, to Ramsden's shooting box. Turn left along a wide track and enjoy splendid views of upper Nidderdale, dominated by Great and Little Whernside, which unfold along the next 4 miles of high level walking, known as Dale Edge. The track

50

finishes at a long-disused coal mine whose deep shaft, though fenced, is best avoided. From here, the line shown by the OS no longer exists, so head south-west, down an obvious path, to join a bulldozed track taking you steeply down to cross Woo Gill ford. Climbing again, on the far side, double back to the right at the wall up a stony track, reaching Firth Plantation on your left after a short distance. Go through the gate and straight ahead for $^3/_4$ mile until another track is reached just above Scar House Reservoir. Turn left and follow it down to cross the dam. In stormy weather, when westerly winds chop the surface of the water, considerable quantities spill down the face of the dam and the spray hangs high above.

After crossing, turn right for 300 yards, then left up a steep stony track towards Middlesmoor. At the top of the hill pass through a gate into a walled lane. As you follow it down, a new view unfolds ahead, that of Gouthwaite reservoir. Middlesmoor (*see* Walk 4) is an attractive huddle of stone houses, but with the added advantage of a high viewpoint. It has a pub, a shop, and a dramatically-sited church. Along the right-hand side of the churchyard is a flagged path leading to a wicket gate. Beyond the gate the path descends to a stone stile, then by way of a gate into the farmyard of Halfway House. Continue straight on through a gate and along the right-hand hedge to a stile in the lower right-hand corner of the field. After crossing it, keep the wall on your right to find the next stile, near a barn. Cross the stile and follow the left-hand wall to emerge on to the road at a wide bend. Turn left immediately, along the signposted path to Lofthouse (*see* Walk 10) crossing a former railway line, now a road, to reach a footbridge over the limestone gorge of the (frequently dry) Nidd. Turn right after the bridge and after 100 yards emerge in Lofthouse.

POINTS OF INTEREST:
The first half of this walk lies in Fountains Earth, and the second in Byland Earth, territories granted to these rival Cistercian monasteries in the 12th century and worked through the creation of dairy farms, known as granges.

REFRESHMENTS:
The Crown Hotel, Lofthouse (tel no: 0423 75206).
The Crown Hotel, Middlesmoor (tel no: 0423 75204).

Walk 22   LOWER COVERDALE   10m (16km)

Maps: OS Sheets Landranger 99; Outdoor Leisure 30.

A gentle walk with few climbs, through spacious, open country.

Start: At 127877, Middleham Market Place.

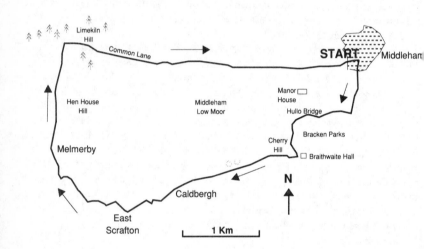

Go through the archway next to the Richard III hotel and at the top of the yard turn right, then left just before the castle. The track skirts the moat and continues to a gate where you go straight ahead, with the wall on your right, to the next gate. Here you change sides and proceed with the wall on your left, turning right after 500 yards (there is no clear path) to head for a distant barn. Turn left here, through the gate, and aim to cross the line of trees on your right about half-way along their length. Continue forward to join a track dropping through woodland to Hullo Bridge. After crossing the beautifully-clear River Cover, flowing here through a miniature limestone gorge, continue to follow the track up the hill, past fields showing clear traces of medieval ridge-and-furrow cultivation and through two gates to join the lane below Braithwaite Hall (*see* Walk 11). Turn right along the lane for ¼ mile, then fork left along the footpath signposted to Caldbergh. Climb slightly to pass above a small plantation, then follow the indistinct path forwards (keeping the barn visible ahead on your right-hand) to pass through three gates in succession. Follow the track as it descends gently to Caldbergh. Turn left here at the footpath sign to East Scrafton and pass between the house and the farm buildings to reach a gate. Go slightly right to find steps leading down to a footbridge. After crossing, keep straight ahead to cross the awkward wooden fence ahead: it is easier further right. Once in the field, keep the wall on your right to find a footbridge over a second stream. Continue, still following the wall, to East Scrafton Hall where you pass through a gate, right, then turn left to another. Go through to a lane. Turn right and cross the Coverham road, taking the path signposted to Melmerby. The path descends by steps to a well-hidden, ruined chapel and continues along the river bank to a footbridge. After crossing, climb through woodland and proceed westwards along its upper edge to a stile. Cross and turn right to join a green lane. Arriving on the Carlton road, turn left, then right at the sign for Melmerby. Turn left at the T-road, then right again to head north up the village street of Melmerby. After crossing the cattle grid turn half right across the moor, as indicated by the footpath sign. The path is faint, but its line is indicated by posts which lead to a stile. Go over and head for a gate in the north corner of the field. On passing through, continue north across a low ridge to find a stile in the far right-hand corner of the field. Go over two more stiles in quick succession, then cross the gallops to emerge on Common Lane. Turn right for $^3/_4$ mile to a T-road, then leave the road and go straight ahead on a signed bridleway for 2 miles of open downland walking, with good views on both sides, to reach the road near Middleham. Turn left and, if the road is busy, avoid the traffic by crossing the stile by the pinfold and following the path behind the road wall back to Middleham (*see* Walk 11) and the start.

REFRESHMENTS:
Many available in Middleham

Walks 23 and 24   **MASHAM AND LEIGHTON**   11m (18km) or 5m (8km)

Maps: OS Sheets Landranger 99; Pathfinder SE 07/17, 27/37 & 28/38.

Pleasant easy walking.

Start: Masham Market Square.

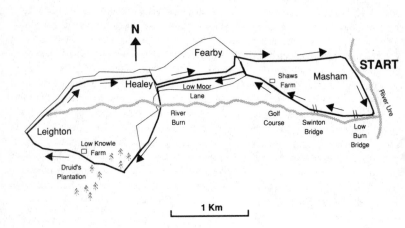

From Masham Market Square go along Silver Street and opposite Brownless Garage take the signposted path to a sports ground where you turn right. Continue by the river, then through a waymarked wood, exiting over a stile. Pass a house and turn left into a surfaced lane. Go along it, passing a lane on the left, and continue along an unsurfaced lane to join a riverside path for ¹/₂ mile to the meeting of the Ure and Burn Rivers. Turn right, crossing a stile into a wood and following the path by the River Burn to Low Burn Bridge. Cross the bridge and then a stile on your right to join a riverside path and continue along it to Masham Golf Course, reached over a stile. Continue along the edge of the golf course to Swinton Bridge. Cross and go through a wicket gate on your left. Pass in front of the club house and continue along a riverside path to the end of the golf course. Exit over a stile, climb the side of a fenced field and go along a gated farm road towards Shaw's Farm, turning right by the outbuildings. Follow waymarkers past the farm, going through a gate and bearing half right, aiming for the middle of some transmission poles seen ahead. Ignoring the gate on your right go through the one ahead and take the path to Micklebury Lane(*). Turn left down the lane and right along Low Moor Lane for 1¹/₂ miles. Turn left at the lane end, cross the River Burn and continue along the road for an uphill road walk of 1¹/₂ miles to where, at the 'No Through Road' symbol, you go right into Knowle Lane and follow a 'Druid's Wood' sign westward for 1 mile to Druid's Plantation. Take the path signposted 'Viewpoint' to a hilltop folly resembling a miniature Stonehenge called the Druid's Temple (*see* Walk 16). Return down Knowle Lane for a few hundred yards and go left first through two gates. Turn left along the edge of the wood and left again through a further gate between plantations. Now go right with Knowle Plantation on your right to join a track going through a gate into a field. Cross this along a track to join a path from Broadmines. Go left along the path to cross Potts Beck on a packhorse bridge and climb steeply out of the valley and through a facing gate. Turn right up the field to an old barn and go right through a gate. Cross the field to exit through a gate into Leighton hamlet. Turn right along the road for 1¹/₂ miles to Healey where, beyond the school, turn right and continue to the junction on your left. Turn into Low Moor Lane, which you walked on the outward route. When, after 1¹/₂ miles, it bifurcates, turn left along Micklebury Lane, passing the spot where the outward route joined it(#). Opposite where a lane branches diagonally on the left go through a gate on the right and follow yellow waymarkers for the final 1¹/₂ miles back to Masham (*see* Walk 1), passing Theakston's Brewery (hardest part of the walk!) and turning left along Red Lane into the Market Square.

For the shorter walk, go right (*) to join the longer route at (#).

REFRESHMENTS:
The Kings Head Hotel, Masham (tel no: 0765 89295).
The Bay Horse Inn, Masham (tel no: 0765 89276).
The Bruce Arms, Masham (tel no: 0765 89372).

REETH AND SURRENDER BRIDGE 13m (21km)
Maps: OS Sheets Landranger 92 and 98; Outdoor Leisure 30.
*Moderate walking on moorland, along field paths and country
lanes.*
Start: Reeth.

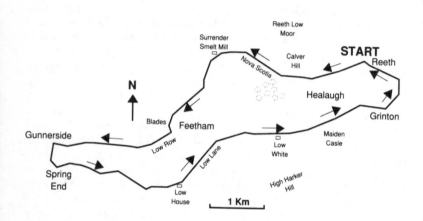

Leave Reeth along the Gunnerside road, B6270, and half-way up School Hill turn
right along signposted Skellgate Lane. At the very end of the lane, go through a gate
on to Reeth Low Moor. Turn left by the wall and beyond its corner go westwards over
moorland with Riddings Farm below on your left. Join a track from the farm, keeping
close to the wall on your left. Cross another stretch of open moor and rejoin a wall on
your left. Calver, 1599ft, is on your right here. Continue westwards along an undefined
route across moorland, bearing left between spoil heaps to go below a cottage called
Moorcock to a farm road. Go right along past Thirns and Nova Scotia on your left and
on to the moor, close to an intake wall. When about 3 miles from Reeth cross a stile in
a facing wall, descend steeply to Cringley Bottom and cross the beck by leaping from
rock to rock. Scramble up the steep far bank on to more moorland where you go half-

left along a narrow track, where you will come first to **Surrender Smelt Mill** then to nearby Surrender Bridge.

Cross the bridge and go uphill along the Langthwaite-Low Row road. Opposite number 4 butt go right along a green track, moving south-west over Feetham Pasture for 1 mile to Blades hamlet, where you go right, along a high level road. When this turns downhill to Smarler, continue straight ahead, first by a wall, then along a plateau, The Barf, above an escarpment. At a gate with a request notice to 'Please Close The Gate' go immediately left along a green track to Gunnerside. Leave it by crossing a bridge over the beck and going left along the B6270 to cross the Swale at Gunnerside New Bridge. A few yards along the road, which goes right and uphill, go through a small gate atop a few steps on your left to reach Dubbing Garth Lane. Turn left along it for 2 miles, skirting the Swale on your left. At The Gables go left along a minor road and, where there is a turning left to Isles Bridge, continue ahead for $^1/_4$ mile to Low Houses, where the road ends. Beyond the few houses, at a signpost to 'Grinton $4^1/_2$ miles', turn left along walled Low Lane for two glorious miles to exit near Low Whita. Turn left along a quiet road to Scabba Wath Bridge. Half a mile further on, turn left through a gate signposted 'Grinton' and follow the waymarkers to the Swale. Take a stiled riverside path to a suspension bridge. Cross and turn right, going diagonally over fields along a clear way. Enter a walled lane through a gate near a barn. Go uphill along it and turn right along a lane back into Reeth.

POINTS OF INTEREST:
Surrender Smelt Mill - A scheduled ancient monument, is a reminder of Swaledale's association with lead mining.

REFRESHMENTS:
Several pubs and cafés in Reeth.
The King's Head, Gunnerside (tel no: 0748 86261). Walkers frequently outnumber the locals here!

Walk 26   WHARFEDALE AND KETTLEWELL   4m (6.5km)

Maps: OS Sheets Landranger 98; Outdoor Leisure 30.

Easy walking, but a number of stiles.

Start: At 967723, park at Townfoot Bridge car park in Kettlewell.

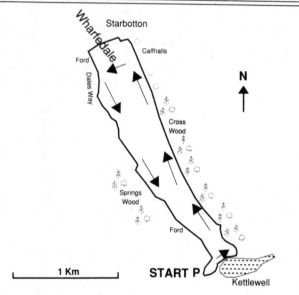

Cross the small bridge into the village and follow the road up the left side of the Bluebell Hotel. Where the road turns right, go straight ahead, over a stile, then turn left along the wall-side. This path follows the route of a Roman road from Ilkley, up Wharfedale over Stake Pass to Bainbridge and on to Catterick. Drystone walls enclose the small fields and there are stiles to be negotiated. The path is more or less level along the lower edge of an old wood, Cross Wood. The track sloping diagonally up the opposite side of the dale led to the Moor End lead mines. At the third barn (Calfhalls) past the wood, angle left down to Starbotton village. Pause to look round the village and note the mullioned cottage with its date stone of 1656. Cross the road, B6160, to a short path to the footbridge, with flood markers. Cross the bridge and follow the well-signposted Dales Way to the left, downstream to Kettlewell. Riverside birds include grey wagtails and sandpipers. Down the dale the overhang of Kilnsey Crag, popular with rock climbers, can be seen. There are numerous rabbits in this area, including black ones.

Take time to explore Kettlewell. A stroll through its quiet lanes and turnings reveals a number of 17th and 18th century cottages. Lovely gardens run down to the beck. The church is late Victorian. There are three inns and various tearooms.

REFRESHMENTS:
The Bluebell, Kettlewell (tel no: 075 676 230). Children and pets welcome.
The Racehorses, Kettlewell (tel no: 075 676 233).

Walk 27   RAYDALE   4m (6.5km)

Maps: OS Sheets Landranger 98; Outdoor Leisure 30.
Easy walking, mainly along field paths and lanes.
Start: At 922876, the Carlow Stone.

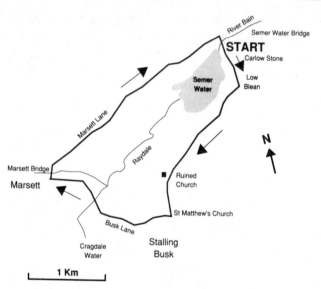

If you stand at the **Carlow Stone** facing the lake, the way is left for $^1/_2$ mile along the road as far as Low Blean Farm, where you turn right over a ladder stile opposite, signposted 'Stalling Bush 1 mile'. Go south-westerly from the stile following yellow markers across pastures, over three stiles, cradled in beautiful countryside, and with Addlebrough (1564ft) at your back. The way is past a barn on your left, close to the lake on your right. As Semer Water slips behind, you climb gradually across rough pasture on a good, signposted path going through three gated stiles to ruinous **Stalling Busk Church**. On leaving the church turn right and straight away go half-left through a gap in a broken wall where a signpost marked 'Stalling Busk' points the way uphill. After $^1/_2$ mile the hamlet of Stalling Busk is reached, perched at the top of a 200ft climb. Once in the hamlet, turn right, then bear left to have a look at the **Church of St Matthew**. From the church bear right to unsignposted Busk Lane opposite and continue along it, descending steeply to cross Cragdale Beck on a concrete bridge. Turn right, keeping close to the beck and make your way across muddy, low-lying ground to a footbridge over Raydale Beck. Continue straight ahead crossing Longdale Sike on a slab bridge, and aim for a stile beside a gate. Go over and along the lane ahead, with Marsett Beck on your right, to the green in Marsett hamlet. Turn right, crossing Marsett Bridge and keep on Marsett Lane, which you have just joined, for a good mile, passing Carr End Farm after $^1/_2$ mile, on your right. The views over **Semer Water** are enchanting and you can pick out the part you have already walked and admire Stalling Busk from a distance. About $^1/_2$ mile past Carr End Farm, where the lane descends, cross the signposted stile on your right and take a route identified by yellow markers for $^1/_4$ mile across a field and by a woodside beck to a gate close to Semer Water Bridge on your right. Turn right here and follow the road skirting the lake back to the Carlow Stone.

POINTS OF INTEREST:

The Carlow Stone – This and the nearby Mermaid Stones are said to have been thrown at each other by the devil and a giant from hills on opposite sides of the lake. Couples thinking about getting married are drawn to the Carlow Stone because tradition has it that touching it will bring prosperity and many children.

Stalling Busk Church – Access to the ruin, with its tilted headstones, is through a slit stile. The church was built in 1603, rebuilt on the same site in 1722 and became disused in 1909.

Church of St Matthew – Built in 1909 to replace the ruined one you have just passed.

Semer Water – The mists of time have shrouded this lake with superstitions and legends, the most famous being that which tells of a town that sank beneath the waters after a poor traveller was refused food and drink by all but one household. *'Semer water rise'*, he cursed, *'Semer water sink! and swallow all save this little house that gave me meat and drink'*.

REFRESHMENTS:

The nearest pubs are in the nearby village of Bainbridge.

Maps: OS Sheets Landranger 92 & 98; Outdoor Leisure 30.
A walk up Gunnerside Gill by the beck side, to the Sir Francis lead mines.
Start: At 952983, in Gunnerside.

Going over the bridge, turn left along a track by the beck, opposite the Kings Head Inn. Follow the track to a Gunnerside Gill sign, turning right up eight steps. Pass through a handgate, bear left to follow the beckside to another handgate to woodland and go through keeping to the path along the beckside. The large boulders around this area were deposited by free flooding over the centuries. Walk about 300 yards to a gated stile on the right and climb the steps. Continue ahead passing a 'Woodland Path' sign into the wood. Follow this path, going over a wooden stile, to where two stone stiles lead into a field. With the wall on your left, go over two more stiles. After a short distance you reach the remains of the Sir Francis mining complex, a worthwhile break point to look and ponder. This site is quiet now, but in the 1800s it was full of activity.

　　Continuing our walk we follow the waymarks in front of the teams. Cross over the stile, go up to a track from the mine on the side of the gill, climb over a wooden stile and walk until you reach a stone stile. At this point, looking across the beck, the ruined buildings you see are those of the mine office and stables. Going over the stile and follow a well-defined track for about $^3/_4$ mile. The ruins you now come to are the Bunting mines, which were formerly the offices, stables, blacksmiths, gunpowder stores and the water wheel pit. Across the valley you can see the Dolly Mine. From this point you follow the beckside for a further $^3/_4$ mile or so to reach the remains of Blakethwaite peat store and smelt mill. Cross the stone slab bridge over the beck and follow the well-defined bridle path that takes you along the side of the valley back towards Gunnerside, passing Lownathwaite mines and Dolly lead level. Follow the path to Dyke Heads, turning left at the track road to reach **Gunnerside**.

POINTS OF INTEREST:
Gunnerside – The name is Norse and means the shieling of Gunner. The lead mining flourished in the 18th and 19th century, in 1851, 180 villagers were employed in the mines at Gunnerside Gill. The Bunting and Lownathwaite mines, comprise one of the richest ore bearing complex in Swaledale.

The fields in this area are some of the oldest enclosures in Swaledale, many of the barns seen on the walk are relics of 18th and early 19th centuries, an era in which many miners had smallholdings on which they kept a few sheep or a cow or two.

REFRESHMENTS:
The Kings Head Inn, Gunnerside (tel no: 0748 86261).
The Tea Shop, Muker (tel no: 0748 86409).
The Kearton Guest House, Thwaite (tel no: 0748 86277).
All welcome walkers and children.

Maps: OS Sheets Landranger 98; Outdoor Leisure 30.
Easy walking up a gradual incline with a short, steep descent.
Start: At 017867, by the village green in West Burton.

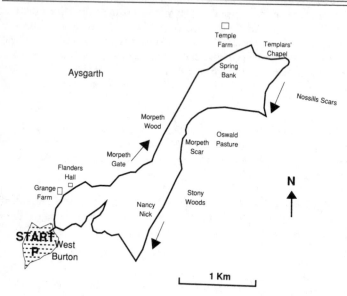

From Burton Bridge, where Walden Beck emerges from a rocky gorge, follow the walled lane past Flanders Hall and Howrane Farm to Morpeth Gate ('gate' being the dialect for road) once the main road from Middleham to Askrigg. After ¹/₂ mile note a finger post to the Templars' Chapel on the left by a tubular steel gate. Go through the gate, and the sheepfold beyond, and go forward in a long, narrow pasture. Proceed along the hillside past a water trough, near the bottom wall, on a narrow, grass-covered track. Where the track divides, take the right branch up the hill to a gate with stone posts. Go through and forward across four pastures with firstly a fence and then a wall on your left. **Bolton Castle** can be seen across the dale. Go over a stile with a lambing gate to a lane. Another stile now leads to the **Templars' Chapel**.

From the lane strike diagonally south-east across the pasture to an iron gate in the high corner between two plantations. Go through the gate to the concrete road which forms the top end of Hargill Lane. Note the packhorse tracks, the old limestone quarries and a lime kiln. Continue up the road, pausing at the top to take in the view. Push on up to the ruined building where the drystone enclosure walls come together to form a lane. Go forward to rejoin Morpeth Gate. Turning right, follow the green road for $^1/_2$ mile to join the Accommodation Road at Morpeth Scar. Follow the rough stony track up to the left. Go forward along a walled lane through a gate to an open pasture, Burton Moor. Go along a cart-track marked 'West Burton' across the next pasture. Ahead is the hidden valley of Walden. Strike downhill north-westerly, via a ranging post, to a stile in the wall below it, then proceed with care down a steep, zig-zag path through the remains of Jack Wood. **Aysgarth** can be seen across the dale. Go over a stile at the bottom and cross a narrow field to another stile. Turn left and follow the wire fence down to **Barrack Wood**. Go down to, and over, a step stile. The path now makes straight for West Burton. Go through a handgate to the left of the field barn. Go forward to another handgate in the wood below the waterfall. At the foot of the second field turn sharp left to a handgate. Go through, down a short, steep path to the packhorse bridge, and join Mill Lane up to **West Burton**.

POINTS OF INTEREST:

Bolton Castle – Mary, Queen of Scots, was a prisoner here. It is open to the public and houses a folk museum.

Templars' Chapel – The Knights Templar established their small monastery on Pen Hill, about 1200AD. Only the ruined chapel remains above ground.

Aysgarth – Famous for its Upper and Lower Falls. The Coach and Carriage Museum is also worth a visit. The church has a wooden screen brought from Jervaulx.

Barrack Wood – Rich in unusual flora including purple loosestrife. Please walk with care here and through the following hay meadows.

West Burton – A picturesque Dales village. The oddly-placed building on the wide green was once an inn.

REFRESHMENTS:

The Palmer Flatt Hotel, Aysgarth (tel no: 096 93 228). On the A684 road.

The Fox and Hounds, West Burton (tel no: 096 93 279). Lunch time bar meals. Children welcome.

Walk 30   KELD AND RAVENSEAT   6m (10km)

Maps: OS Sheets Landranger 98; Outdoor Leisure 30.

Moderate walking along field and fell paths with some road walking.

Start: The bottom end of Keld hamlet.

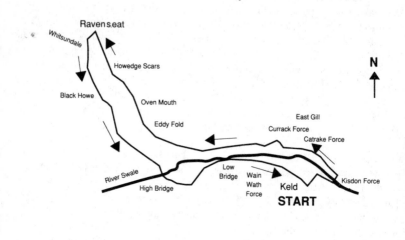

Leave the bottom end of Keld along Keld Lane, signposted 'Public Footpath to Muker' and after $1/4$ mile, at a double Pennine Way sign, go left, downhill, to the footbridge over the Swale. Here detour downstream for about 300 yards to Kisdon Force, one of Swaledale's finest waterfalls. Retrace your steps to the bridge. Cross the Swale and continue uphill with East Gill Force on your right and turn left along a path signposted 'East Stonesdale Farm'. Turn left above the farm, going along a bridleway for $1/2$ mile through beautiful countryside with tantalising glimpses of Catrake Force and Currack Force. When the Tan Hill road is reached, cross it, go through a gate showing a footpath sign and walk along the top of Cotterby Scar, following markers, for about $3/4$ mile. There are good views of Wain Wath Force along this section. Where the scar ends, go right along a farm road to empty Smithy Holme Farm. There go half-right across open moor, aiming for a 'Ravenseat–Keld' signpost. Continue, passing on your right Eddy Fold, a large sheepfold, guided by yellow markers, passing close to the edge of Oven Mouth and Howe Edge ravines. Upstream of these two narrow gorges the way descends pleasantly through pastures to the twin farms of **Ravenseat**.

At the first house turn left along a track and cross an ancient packhorse bridge over Whitsundale Beck. Go up the road, past a house called Black Howe, ignoring a signpost saying 'Footpath to Hoggarth Bridge'. Just beyond the house go left by the moor wall. Go over a stile, passing, on your left, two barns, to cross another stile in the same wall. Go south-east on an undefined way down a boggy, rough pasture and then through a gap in a ruinous corner wall. Continue downhill, crossing a pasture, then a stile in the wall on your left. Go past another barn, over a waymarked stile and across another field to the B6270. Turn left along it, crossing the Swale at High Bridge, and continue along the road, with fine views of Wain Wath Force, Rainby Force and Currack Force, for the $1^1/_2$ miles back to Keld.

POINTS OF INTEREST:
Ravenseat – A former drover trading post with eleven households, a chapel and a pub.

REFRESHMENTS:
Unfortunately there are neither pubs nor cafés on this walk. So bring your own and if you don't like what's on offer you only have yourself to blame!

Walk 31   KISDON FORCE   6m (10km)

Maps: OS Sheets Landranger 98; Outdoor Leisure 30.

One of the most popular walks in Upper Swaledale. Not to be missed.

Start: Keld.

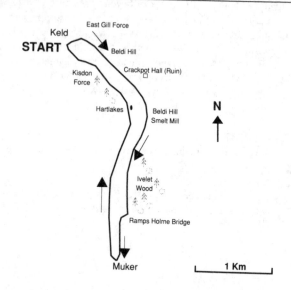

From Keld take the footpath at the bottom of the village signposted to Muker and after ¼ mile, where there is a Pennine Way sign, go left, down a wooded, hillside path and through a gate to cross the river Swale on a footbridge. Continue, going uphill with East Gill Force, a triple waterfall, on your right to join a track at a point where Pennine Way and Coast to Coast Walk meet. The Pennine Way goes left, but your way is right, eastwards, over a bridge above the falls, through a gate and along a stony track contouring the side of Beldi Hill. From here there are terrific views of Swaledale's highest point, Great Shunner Fell (2340ft), and Keld, its highest village. Continue along this high level track, which curves over an arched bridge at Swinner Gill, with its reminders of Swaledale's lead mining connections. Keep on the main track, going steeply downhill by East Wood and through a gate to the foot of the gill. Cross a footbridge beside Beldi Hill Smelt Mill and continue for $1\frac{1}{2}$ miles along a stony stretch which becomes a pleasant riverside green track, springy and easy on the feet. Soon the track, now stony again, goes left, uphill, towards Ramps Holm Bridge over the Swale. Cross and turn right along a track signposted 'Muker'. Go left over a narrow stile and along a clear path through meadows into picturesque Muker, a good butty stop. On entering the village you pass Stoneleigh on your right. On leaving, go to the left of Stoneleigh along the Kisdon Road to just beyond a bungalow called 'Breconside' where the unsurfaced road branches left for Kisdon. Continue straight ahead through a metal corner gate and follow an enclosed path northwards. Go through three gates, beyond which a green path leads to a barn with a signpost to Keld. Go ahead, over stiles, following yellow markers, and through a wooden gate to the riverside path. Walk upstream for $\frac{1}{2}$ mile, then go half-left, aiming for a waymarked stile near a ruined wall. Follow the waymarkers across stiled fields, passing a derelict farm, **Hartlakes**, on your right. The way is now uphill along a sunken, low-walled path and through a gate into **Kisdon Force** Wood. The path climbs steadily to a footpath sign where the Pennine Way is joined. Go westwards along it back into Keld.

POINTS OF INTEREST:

Hartlakes – Known locally as 'Boggles House' because it is haunted.
Kisdon Force – Thought by many to be Swaledale's best waterfall. A detour can be made from the Bridge at the start of the walk simply by going downstream for a little way. Well worth the effort.

REFRESHMENTS:

The Farmer's Arms, Muker (tel no: 0748 86297).
The Muker Tea Shop (tel no: 0748 86409).

Walk 32   CLAPHAM   6¹/₂m (10.5km)

Maps: OS Sheets Landranger 98; Outdoor Leisure 2.

An upland walk along quiet tracks, with breathtaking views and many interesting geological features.

Start: At 745692, the National Park Centre car park in Clapham.

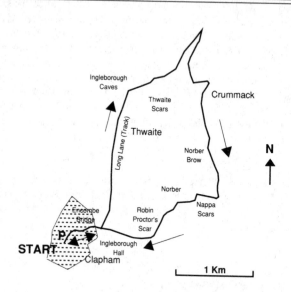

Turn right on leaving the car park, taking the road towards the church. Just before the church take the lane to your right, passing through two short, dark tunnels. Take the first left turn and follow the walled lane. Ahead and to the right are Thwaite Scars, while the hill on your left is **Ingleborough**. Just over 1 mile along lane you will see, below you and to the left, the entrance to Ingleborough Cave.

At the end of the lane follow a less distinct path half-right and cross the ladder stile. Approximately 100 yards further on, the path bears left. As you reach a stretch of limestone pavement on your left the dramatic mass of **Pen-y-Ghent** appears ahead of you. Another bridleway soon joins from the right. Turn along this, descend to Crummackdale Farm and follow the walled Crummack Lane. After 1¹/₂ miles take the path to your right, signposted Norber. Pass along the cliffs of Nappa Scars and, a little

70

further on, to your right, you will see the **Norber Erratics**. After exploring them, return to the path and follow it past Robin Proctor's Scar. The path runs alongside a drystone wall and then diagonally across a field, passing a dried-up mere, to a ladder stile. Turn right along another walled lane which will take you back to your original path from **Clapham**. Retrace the outward route to the start.

POINTS OF INTEREST:

Ingleborough and Pen-y-Ghent – The walk has wonderful views of two of Yorkshire's famous 'Three Peaks', 2372ft and 2277ft high respectively.

Norber Erratics – These are boulders that were carried along Crummackdale by a melting glacier and deposited on Norber Brow. Other features of limestone scenery are seen to great effect on this walk – the bare grey rocks of the scars, the shake holes along the side of Ingleborough and a stretch of limestone pavement.

Clapham – A delightful village, with a pretty wooded beck running through it. The naturalist Reginald Farrar lived here, as did, reputedly, the 'Witch of Clapham'.

REFRESHMENTS:
The New Inn, Clapham (tel no: 04685 203).

Walks 33 and 34   **HARDRAW FORCE**   7m (11km) or 4m (6.5km)
Maps: OS Sheets Landranger 98; Outdoor Leisure 30.
A splendid walk along field and fell paths with some steep climbs.
Map and compass may be needed on the fells.
Start: The National Park Centre car park, Hawes.

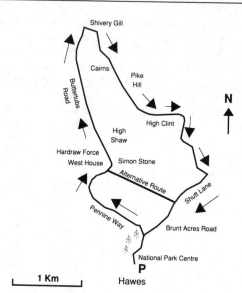

From the National Park Centre cross the disused railway line and take the path to
the Brunt Acres Road. Turn right for 75 yards. Now follow a path on your left
marked 'Pennine Way', crossing two fields diagonally on paved stones to rejoin the
road. Continue north along the road, crossing the River Ure and about ¼ mile further
on, where the road climbs, turn left over a stile at a 'Pennine Way' signpost. Take the
paved path westward, over stiles and through pastures, reaching Hardraw village
opposite the Green Dragon Inn. Detour here through the inn, for a small charge, and
go up either side of Fossdale Beck to spectacular **Hardraw Force**. Back at the inn
go left through the back yard of the end cottage and climb the steep, flagged path up
a field. Here the views of Upper Wensleydale are excellent and embrace Yorburgh
(1686ft) and Wether Fell (2015ft). When you reach the top of the field cross a stile, then

72

climb again along a fenced path to West House, where you turn right through a gated stile.

The shorter alternative route of 4 miles takes the path from here to the hilltop hamlet of Simonstone and continues through a series of stiled fields to Sedbusk, rejoining the main route there.

From West House the main route goes up the farm track to the Buttertubs Road and left along it to a signpost indicating 'Shaw Sill Wood'. Go down the enclosed path and cross a footbridge to explore enchanting Sylvan Shaw Gill and its waterfalls. Upstream, cross another footbridge and turn left, then right, through a wall. Go right down a lane to a hamlet of High Shaw and back to the Buttertubs Road. Turn left along this unfenced moorland road for 2 miles of marvellous uphill walking, framed by stunning views. When, just past Shivery Gill on the right, a bridleway signposted 'Sedbusk 2$^1/_2$ miles' is reached, turn right and climb steeply on to Abbotside Common. The way, at first, is undefined: go right over deep, rocky Shivery Gill and continue in a south-easterly direction along Pike Hill which, at 1700ft above sea level, will thrill you with panoramic views that enfold the fells of Great Shunner, Wether, Dodd and Widdale with distant Ingleborough and Whernside thrown in for good measure. Continue along the escarpment, keeping well to the left of four clearly seen cairns. As you pass them wheel eastwards, keeping well back from steep Hill Clint. At the eastern end of the escarpment descend to join a track which will take you through a gate, half-left across a pasture. Go through another gate and down a sunken track to a walled enclosure with trees. Turn right by the trees, go down a rutted track and over a stile into Shutt Lane. Go right, along the walled lane for $^1/_4$ mile into the hamlet of Sedbusk. The shorter route rejoins here. At the bottom of the hamlet go right along the road. Cross the stile on your left signposted 'Haylands Bridge' and cross stiled fields to the Hardraw–Askrigg Road. Cross and go over a stile to follow another signposted path over more stiled fields. Go over a hump-back bridge then another field to reach the Brunt Acres Road. Turn left along it back into Hawes.

POINTS OF INTEREST:
Hardraw Force – At 96 feet the highest waterfall in England.

REFRESHMENTS:
The Green Dragon, Hardraw (tel no: 09697 392).
There is also a café-shop in Hardraw.
Lots of hotels, pubs and cafés in Hawes.

Walk 35 ASCENT OF GREAT COUM 7½m (11.5km)

Maps: OS Sheets Landranger 98; Outdoor Leisure 2.
A fine upland walk with some easy climbing.
Start: At 704870, the car park in Dent.

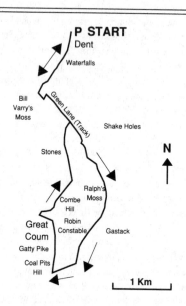

Leave the car park and cross the main road to a lane opposite. Follow it to a green area and pass this, following the lane past some delightful whitewashed cottages. The lane leads to a stony path which heads up Flinter Gill. Follow this steep stony track upwards to a gate. Pass through and continue heading upward. Eventually the track leads to a gate which marks the beginning of the moorland: the track also becomes walled at this point. Walk up the walled track to meet a similar track running across it (this old road runs from Barbondale Road to Ingleton). Turn left at this junction to follow the old road. The fine views over Dentdale make this walk along the lane a worthwhile journey, despite the varying conditions underfoot. When a track is reached running up from Deepdale keep with the right-hand track as it heads upwards on a high-level traverse of Deepdale. When you are opposite the waterfalls of Gastack Beck at the head of Deepdale, look for a small wooden gate in the wall on your right, approximately

74

100 yards before a metal gate across the track. Go through this gate and head half-left (south-west)) across the moor to reach a stone wall. Follow the wall up on to the ridge to meet a cross wall running along the top of the ridge. Turn right at this wall to follow it as it rises to Gatty Pike, noticing, on the way, the large County Stone situated where the wall running up from Long Gill joins the ridge wall.

From the cairn on Gatty Pike there are excellent views of Whernside, just across the valley, and of Ingleborough to the right. From Gatty Pike continue following the ridge wall, crossing an incoming wall from the right and a small rocky outcrop. The wall reaches a corner created by its right-angled turn left and a wall running from the right. Negotiate the wall, which has no stile, and turn left to follow the original wall once more. After about 100 yards another junction of walls is negotiated to reach the summit cairn of **Great Coum**. Leave the summit to rejoin the wall previously crossed. Turn left to follow the wall descending the moor. Cross an incoming wall from the left and continue with the wall as it further descends the moor. When it turns to the left to head in a northerly direction keep with it. When it turns once more to descend the moor more steeply, leave its confines to head in the same direction (north) across the moor to reach the **Megger Stones**. From the Megger Stones head northwards down the moor to locate a wall corner. Follow the right-hand wall down to the walled track and turn left to retrace your way back to Dent via Flinter Gill.

POINTS OF INTEREST:
Great Coum – The highest point of the walk at 2250ft. From the summit there are extensive views of the Lakeland skyline to the north-west and of the closer Howgills to the north. Below the full length of Dentdale can be seen.

Megger Stones – An area of scree on to which many cairns have been built. An excellent high level view of Dent.

REFRESHMENTS:
Dent is blessed with an abundance of refreshments, alcoholic or otherwise.

Walk 36   THWAITE, MUKER AND KELD   7¹/₂m (11.5km)

Maps: OS Sheets Landranger 92 & 98; Outdoor Leisure 30.

High level walking and riverside paths.

Start: The village of Thwaite.

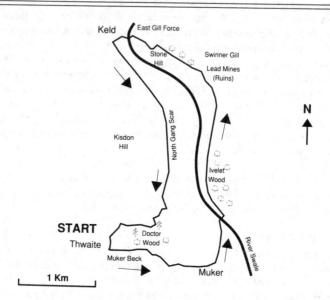

Take the lane eastwards past the front of the guest house and follow the Pennine Way behind a farmhouse at the end of the village. After a few yards pass through a stile into a field. Follow the path, keeping Muker Beck on the right, and head for two stiles. Go between a barn and an electricity pole. Go over two more stiles and bear left over a small bridge. Go over a wall stile and keep the wall on your right to another stile. Bear right to a large barn, pass in front of it and head for a stile on to the beck side. Follow the path to a road, and follow this to **Muker**. Bear left past the village store, passing the church and the public hall to the right. Bear right and turn left down a snicket to a sign, 'Footpath to Gunnerside'. Follow this path over several stiles to reach the river bank.

Turn right and over a stile and footbridge. Climb steps and turn left up a steep rise. Turn left uphill and when the path joins a well-defined track, follow it for about 2 miles to a small footbridge near the ruined smelt mill, behind which is a waterfall. Go through the gate and climb up the steep track through another gate. The track now falls gently to another gate. Walk a few yards and leave the track to join the Pennine Way. Cross East Gill Force over the bridge, bear right, and climb a short rise to a handgate. A Pennine Way sign indicates **Keld**, which is only a short way right. Our walk goes to the left. Go through a gate at the end of a wall lane and climb gently between two small hummocks. Bear right past a pile of stones and a Pennine Way sign. Continue ahead through a gap in the wall near a Pennine Way sign. Follow the footpath by the wallside and climb gradually. Care is required on this part of the walk, it is often muddy and rocky. Pause to look across at Swinner Gill, with the ruined Beldi Hill lead smelting mill at the foot of it, before following the path which levels out, following the flank of Kisdon Hill. Go over a stile, then another to reach a gate. After two wall gaps, a gentle climb and a series of stiles, head down towards a derelict house and Pennine Way sign. Turn right and head for a small barn, take the path westwards through a gate and down to Kisdon House. Continue through a second gate and around the back of the house. After a few yards turn left near a Pennine Way sign. After passing a calf house on the right, bear half-right and head for a stile. Continue downhill towards another stile and a Pennine Way sign. Follow the wall to the field bottom and turn right towards a gate and small bridge. Cross the bridge and a field, then go through a gate back to **Thwaite**.

POINTS OF INTEREST:

Muker, Keld and Thwaite – The names are of Norse origin. Two famous naturalists, Cherry and Richard Kearton, were born at Thwaite. Muker has a cluster of charming cottages. The parish church was built in 1580 as a chapel of ease for the larger church at Grinton which until that time had served the whole of Swaledale.

REFRESHMENTS:

Kearton Guest House, Thwaite (tel no: 0748 86277). Welcomes everyone.

BUCKDEN PIKE 7¹/₂m (11.5km)

Maps: OS Sheets Landranger 98; Outdoor Leisure 30

A strenuous ascent, boggy along the ridge, but the rest is easy to moderate.

Start: At 942773, the car park in Buckden.

From the car park at **Buckden**, go through the gate and follow the stony track up Buckden Rakes. This was once the main road over to Wensleydale. The track goes through Rakes Wood, and in spring, creamy tassels of bird cherry overhang it. At the corner, pause to look at the view down to **Hubberholme**. The track curves to the right and up to a gate. Go through and on to the next gate. Here, follow the direction of the finger post diagonally to the right and up to a gate in the drystone wall. The hamlet of Gray is down to the left. In front, the B6160 road goes over Kidstones Pass to Bishopdale. The track winding over the hill to the left goes to Semer Water. From the gate, follow the path to a gateway just below the rocky hillside. Go through and along the path to another gateway and then up to the right across a pasture. Go through the small gate, with finger post, and up to a boggy plateau. Pick your way with care across this, going via a ranging post to a finger post up to the left by a wall. Follow the wall up a short, steep climb, to the summit with cairn and trig point. There is usually a fresh breeze here. If the weather is clear, there are fine views down Wharfedale and across to Langstrothdale. From the summit go over the ladder stile and turn to the right along the wall. From here to Walden Gate, passing the **Memorial Cross**, is is about a mile of usually boggy ground. There are peat hags over to the left, and the fluffy seedheads of bog cotton. Go through the small gate in the wall to the right. This is Walden Road, the old packhorse track. Take care where the limestone is worn smooth. The path descends, becoming a rough track, then a walled lane. On the hill to the left can be seen the remains of a lead smelting chimney. Descend to **Starbotton**, go left along the B6160 to the end of the village, turn right at the finger post and go down the little lane to the footbridge. Go over, turn right and follow the Dales Way upstream. Sandpipers and grey wagtails are to be seen, and in summer there are bellflowers. The path leaves the river and crosses fields to a plantation whose trees include Norwegian maple, copper beech and Wellingtonia. A few yards past the building, a finger post indicates the way back to the riverside. Follow this to an opening in the wall. Go through, turn right over the packhorse bridge and go up the lane to Buckden.

POINTS OF INTEREST:
Buckden – Stone-built houses cluster round a small village green. Buckden was originally the residence of the Forest officials in charge of the hunting preserve of Langstrothdale Chase.
Hubberholme – The church has one of only two surviving rood lofts in Yorkshire. It is roofed with lead from the Buckden mines.
Memorial Cross – A plane crashed here in January 1942. Of the six Polish airmen only one survived. With a broken leg, he crawled down to Starbotton, following a fox's tracks through the snow.
Starbotton – In 1686 the worst recorded flood in Wharfedale engulfed this village. The Georgian houses were built during the development of the lead mining industry.

REFRESHMENTS:
The Buck Inn, Buckden (tel no: 075 676 227).
There are also two tearooms in the village.

Maps: OS Sheets Landranger 98; Outdoor Leisure 30.

A moderate walk with a steady climb along a Roman road and a steep descent to Semer Water.

Start: At 935904, Bainbridge village green.

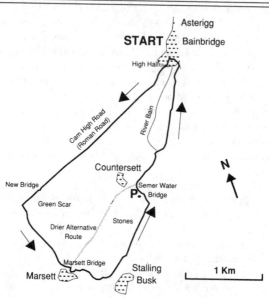

From the village green follow the road signposted for Burtersett, Semer Water and Marsett for $^1/_2$ mile. When the road bends to the left take the walled green lane ahead – the Roman Cam High Road. Follow this through glorious Wensleydale scenery for just over 2 miles. As you pass Green Scar, take the path to your left, signposted 'Marsett'. The path goes through a gate and runs alongside a small area of limestone scar and a derelict drystone wall. Ignoring the more obvious green path going off to your right, make for the ladder stile half left and follow the path to the bottom of the hill. Take the metalled track left through a gate and on to the main road.

    If you wish to avoid the boggy section of the walk, turn left along the road and follow it as far as Semer Water Bridge. Otherwise, turn right into Marsett. Go left after crossing the bridge and left again along the footpath marked Semer Water and Stalling

Busk. Ahead of you is the flat-topped hill of Addlebrough. Cross the footbridge and summon all your resourcefulness and athleticism to get you from one dry patch to another along the next few yards of the path. Another footbridge, to your left, takes you across the next stream. Over this bridge the path goes left alongside a wall. After 50 yards go through the gap in the wall and continue left across a boggy field. Just past the small stone barn, cross the stile to your left. The worst of the mud is now behind you.

Continue straight ahead past a ruined church and along the banks of Semer Water (*see* Walk 27). Cross the ladder stile on to the main road and follow it left past the Carlow and Mermaid's Stones (*see* Walk 27) to Semer Water Bridge. Take the footpath to your right (or left for those who have taken the dry option) signposted 'Bainbridge' and follow the banks of the River Bain, said to be the shortest river in England. When the path becomes indistinct after leaving the bank and crossing a ladder stile, make for the narrow gap in the wall ahead of you. From the top of the hill the lovely view of Askrigg is one familiar to anyone who has watched 'All Creatures Great and Small'. On reaching the road turn left and follow it back to **Bainbridge**.

POINTS OF INTEREST:
Bainbridge – From the 1st to the 4th centuries Bainbridge was an important Roman town and the site of a fort. The village has many reminders of the past, including the stocks on the village green and the tradition of horn-blowing which dates back to when it stood at the edge of the forest of Wensleydale.

REFRESHMENTS:
The Rose and Crown, Bainbridge (tel no: 0969 50225).

ASKRIGG AND WORTON 8m (13km)

Maps: OS Sheets Landranger 98; Outdoor Leisure 30.

A delightful field and woodland walk in Herriot Country with some steep climbs on the waterfall section.

Start: At Askrigg.

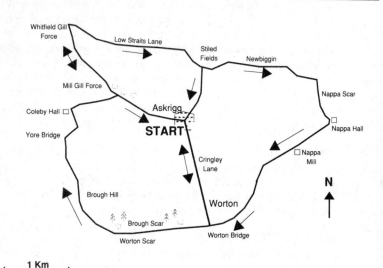

Leave Askrigg along **Cringley Lane**, opposite the Market Cross, signposted 'Footpath Aysgarth–Worton Bridge'. Where the lane turns left, go through a stile on your right and cross a field to the dismantled Wensleydale Railway. Go left along it briefly and descend some steps on your right. Take the flagged path across three stiled fields to Worton Bridge, which cross over the River Ure, and continue steeply uphill to Worton. Turn right along the A684 and almost opposite a bus shelter go through a gate signposted 'Footpath to Bainbridge'. Go half-right up a field to a signposted stile below a wooded bank. Climb steeply through the wood, going westwards along Worton Scar for almost $^1/_2$ mile and on leaving the wood continue westwards across stiled fields with a wall and a wood on your right. Cross a signposted stile in the wall on your right, descend stiled fields to the Semer Water road and go right along it to Bainbridge (*see*

Walk 38). Go through the village, northwards, along the Askrigg road, cross the River Ure using Yore Bridge and continue along a stiled, paved path across a field on your right. Turn left between the abuttments of a railway bridge and cross a packhorse bridge. Go half-right along a path behind Grange Cottage and over two stiles to a road. Turn left in front of Grange Cottage and turn right up a cul-de-sac just before Grange Bridge. Climb steeply past Gill Gate Farm on your right and where the road turns left, turn right at a stile signposted 'Mill Gill'. Continue eastwards over two stiled fields to a signposted path to Mill Gill Force, a 70ft high waterfall in a wooded gorge. Retrace your steps to the sign and follow the signs down Mill Gill to Askrigg to complete a shortened version of the walk. Alternatively, follow the numerous yellow markers for a mile-long scramble upstream to Whitfield Gill Force, a 58ft high waterfall. Now, follow the signpost directions to Low Straits Lane, bearing right, down the gill, to cross a footbridge and climb a steep wooded path. At its top, cross a stile into Low Straits Lane. Go eastwards along this for a mile and when it reaches the Muker–Askrigg road turn right, downhill, to Askrigg. Alternatively, at the 'Askrigg' sign cross a ladder stile on your left and cross stiled fields, eastwards, to Newbiggin. The way is now between Margaret's and George's Cottages and through a white facing gate, still going eastwards, along a path through stiled fields to Nappa Scar. Turn left along the road for 150 yards and take the signposted path to **Nappa Hall**, where you turn right through a gate and take the track diagonally over two fields to the end of Thwaite Holme Lane. Go along this to Nappa Mill. Go right through a gate and cross two footbridges to join the riverside route to Worton Bridge. Complete the circular by returning to Askrigg along the route taken on the outward journey.

POINTS OF INTEREST:
Cringley Lane – Cringley House is used as the exterior of Skeldale House, the TV home and surgery of James Herriot.
Nappa Hall – A fortified farmhouse, built in 1459.

REFRESHMENTS:
There are several pubs in Askrigg.

Walk 40   GREEN SCAR TOP   8¹/₂m (13.5km)

Maps: OS Sheets Landranger 98; Outdoor Leisure 30.

Short steep climbs interspersed with easier stretches to reach high ridge.

Start: At 876899, the Yorkshire Dales National Park Centre, Hawes.

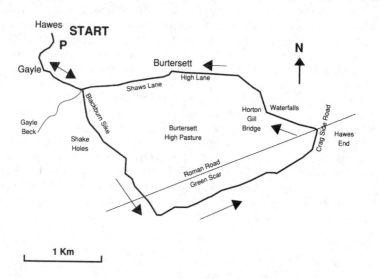

Walk into the town centre and look for the footpath, signposted as the Pennine Way, to Gayle leaving the main street on the south-side through an arch. The path climbs past the parish church and continues as a paved 'causey' above Gayle Beck. Note the distinctive shape of Yorburgh, to your left, as it may well prove useful later. On reaching the Gayle road turn left into the village and cross the bridge before turning left towards Bainbridge (*see* Walk 38). After a few yards only, turn right through a gap stile, signposted to Marsett. The path is not always distinct on the ground, but heads directly towards Yorburgh's craggy summit. Go through two gap stiles to reach a ladder stile. Immediately after crossing it turn right, heading due south, up the hill. A southerly line is maintained – with small diversions to ease the gradient on the steepest slopes – until

Blackburn Sike is reached. After following the stream past the shake holes turn half-left and cross it, heading south-east. There is no clear path just here, but aim to cross the skyline about $1/4$ mile west of Yorburgh summit. At this point you cross a stile and, turning right, join a clear bridleway which has come from Burtersett. Follow the way southwards to the next wall, but after passing through the gate continue forwards when the track goes right, following a footpath which crosses the **Roman road** at a pair of gap stiles by a signpost to Marsett.

Go forward for 100 yards to join the bridleway along Green Scar, turning left along this splendid high-level track, which aims for the prominent scarp of Addlebrough. When Semer Water comes into view, start to descend on a well-made track, crossing the band of limestone to arrive at the road above Countersett. Turn left and follow the road around Hawes End. As it starts to descend take the footpath across the stile to your right, signposted to Horton Gill Bridge. This crosses the Roman road again. Turn right across the bridge and follow the road down to Burtersett. On entering the village, where the road turns right, take the turning to the left, going straight ahead at the junction soon after along a walled track signposted to Gayle. When the track ends at a large barn, continue forward past numerous field barns, through a series of gap stiles until, 1 mile from Burtersett, you reach a familiar ladder stile and rejoin the outward route. From this point it is only 1 mile more back to Hawes.

POINTS OF INTEREST:
Roman road – This ran from Lancaster by way of Ingleton to the fort at Brough-by-Bainbridge.

The names of the hamlets or villages on the walk have Scandinavian origins, since Marsett, Countersett and Burtersett all incorporate the Old Norse element 'saetr', meaning a mountain pasture or a shieling.

REFRESHMENTS:
A wide variety of pubs and cafés is found in Hawes.

Walk 41   ADDLEBROUGH CIRCUIT   9m (14km)

Maps: OS Sheets Landranger 98; Outdoor Leisure 30.

Easy walking, visiting uplands which are now remote but which were desirable and well-populated in prehistory.

Start: At 952911, the car park at the east end of Askrigg.

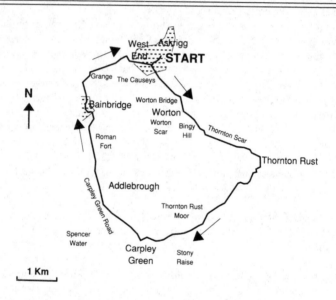

On leaving the car park turn left, then left again immediately over a footbridge. Aim diagonally right up the field, to a stile in the top right-hand corner. Go over it and continue diagonally across two more fields, by way of stiles, before dropping on to a track serving new houses. Turn left for a few yards, then left again at the junction (footpath signpost to Worton). After 100 yards leave the obvious footpath (which bends left) in favour of that going straight ahead through the gate. On following it, Worton village becomes visible ahead, and the path becomes clear as it descends. Go over a number of stiles to reach a delightful stone-flagged **'causey'** leading to the road at Worton bridge. Cross the river and fork left at the village centre to reach the A684. Turn left for 50 yards, then take the stile on the right and walk diagonally left across the field to find the first of eight stiles, which lead forward in a more or less straight line to finish in woodland. The path climbs steeply through Worton Scar to emerge on the road. Turn left and enjoy an easy walk with good views into the dale bottom. Reach Thornton Rust and turn right opposite the village hall. Keep left on crossing the stream and follow the walled bridleway up to a plateau with excellent views back into Wensleydale and forward to Addlebrough hill. At the lane end, aim for a point just left of Addlebrough to find the first gate, then continue on the same bearing along a fairly distinct track to pass through a gate in a cross wall, then one in the wall on your right. Go through two more wall gaps while climbing to the southern shoulder of Addlebrough. At least three prehistoric settlement sites, Stony Raise being the most visible, can be seen from this route. These were, perhaps, associated with a hill fort on the summit. Join the lane by Carpley Green farm and turn right following it down, with views of Semer Water and Green Scar, towards Bainbridge (*see* Walk 38). Avoid the last $^1/_4$ mile of road by crossing the stile on the left at the footpath sign, and turning right down the field on a path close to the road, giving a good view of the Roman fort on the hill ahead. Join the A684 and turn left into the village, using the path across the green which keeps close to the houses on your right. The path emerges on the road to Askrigg, which you follow to the Ure bridge, leaving it on the far side by a footpath on your right signposted to Askrigg. After one field turn left along the beck, crossing it by an old bridge up-stream, and follow a flagged **causey** to the road. Turn right, then cross a stile left in 50 yards, proceeding diagonally forwards to find a stile in the cross wall. Go over a succession of stiles taking you directly to Mill Gill. Cross the footbridge and turn right to gain the last of the stone causeys, leading back to Askrigg. Return to the car park by taking the lane opposite the Market Cross, turning left at the end, and rejoining the outward route.

POINTS OF INTEREST:
The Causeys – Built to provide a dry way to market or mill. They date mainly from the 18th century.

REFRESHMENTS:
Numerous available in Askrigg.

Walk 42   ASKRIGG AND CARPERBY   9m (14.5km)

Maps: OS Sheets Landranger 98; Outdoor Leisure 30.

A superb scenic walk that shows Herriot Country to advantage.

Start: In Askrigg.

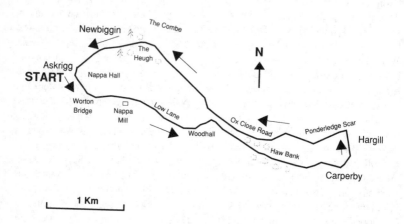

Leave Askrigg along Cringley Lane, opposite the Market Cross, on a footpath signposted 'Aysgarth–Worton Bridge'. Where the lane turns left go sharp right over a narrow stile beside a gate. Cross a field to the dismantled Wensleydale Railway and go left along it for a short distance. Go through a rusty kissing gate and follow a flagged path diagonally south-east across stiled fields to the River Ure at Worton Bridge. Do not cross the bridge. Instead, turn left along the road and where it bends cross a signposted stile, right, and take the riverside track to Nappa Mill. Continue along the farm road to a triple footpath sign near a stone bridge at the end of Thwaite Holme Lane. Cross a stile and turn right along a field to a corner stile to the disused railway. Cross and go over a metal ladder stile. Turn right, parallel to the old track. Some 200 yards past a railway bridge, just beyond a footpath sign, cross a stile, right, and continue eastwards along the railway track to a kissing gate on your left. Continue half-right over

88

stiled fields to West End Farm. Go along Low Lane through Woodhall to the Askrigg–Carperby road at the far end of the hamlet. Turn right for $1/_2$ mile, and at a 'Parking Place' sign, cross Eller Beck on stepping stones and go over a stile signposted 'Carperby'. Bear right and take the path through a hazel wood, continuing eastwards along it over a series of stiles to Carperby football field. Turn left, then right, leaving through a gate near a notice 'Private – No Footpath Beyond This Point' and turn right down a track to the road. Go through **Carperby** as far as the village hall and turn left up Hargill Lane. Where it bifurcates go left through a red metal gate and along a broad bridleway, westwards, to Carperby Stone Mine where stone flags were quarried. Continue westerly on a green track through a red gate to join the **Ox Close Road.** Continue past Wet Groves lead mine below Ivy Scar, to reach a gate. Beyond, ford Eller Beck and turn left along a track which goes left through a gate. After a few yards turn left up a steep, stony track and go through a gate at the top. Keep climbing steadily along a clear high level route, following markers and signposts for more than 1 mile, to reach an isolated house, The Heugh. Turn right, briefly, here along walled Heugh Lane to a wall stile on your left. Cross and go diagonally down two stiled fields into a small wood. At the bottom of this cross stiled pastures to Newbiggin hamlet. Now go down a walled lane beside a barn marked 'Horrabank' and at the second stone barn go left over a narrow stile near a gate and continue south-west across stiled fields, following markers, downhill into Askrigg.

POINTS OF INTEREST:

Carperby – Has a rather splendid 17th century market cross at its western end. The local pub, the Wheatsheaf, is where James Herriot and his wife, Helen, spent their honeymoon in 1941.

Ox Close Road – was frequently used by Lady Anne Clifford travelling between Bolton Castle and Pendragon Castle in Mallerstang. It is often referred to as Lady Anne's Way and much of it follows the route of the old Roman road.

REFRESHMENTS:

The Kings Arms Hotel, Askrigg (tel no: 0969 50258).
The Crown Inn, Askrigg (tel no: 0969 50298).
The Wheatsheaf, Carperby (tel no: 09693 216).

Walk 43   MELBECKS AND BROWNSEY MOORS   9m (14.5km)

Maps: OS Sheets Landranger 92 & 98; Outdoor Leisure 30.

Moderate walking with a very steep climb along some of the best upland ways of Swaledale.

Start: At the Kings Head, Gunnerside.

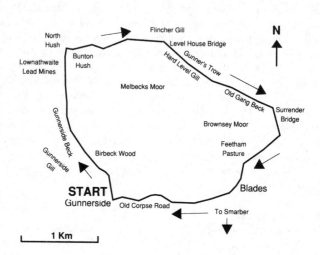

Leave Gunnerside (*see* Walk 28) along the signed footpath to Gunnerside Gill, opposite the Kings Head, and follow the beck northwards to a white gate where you turn right and climb eight steps. Go through a gate and continue past Gunnerside School, now a private residence, on your left. Follow yellow waymarkers through a small gate to a wooded beckside path. Walk upstream to exit through a small gate on your right and go uphill along a waymarked pasture path parallel to the wooded beckside on your left to some lead mining ruins. Beyond, cross a corner fence stile. Bear right up a path through bracken, then go left along a level path close to a wall on your right. Continue to a stile in the wall. Go over and take the clear path that climbs up Gunnerside Gill with the beck on your left. The track levels out opposite Botcher Gill, left, and below Swina Bank Scar, right. Keep to the path for a further mile to reach Bunton Level, which is unsafe to explore. Some 200 yards further on, at a cairn, turn right and take a green track to Bunton Hush, directly above Bunton Level. Turn left up the Y-shaped hush, a steep scramble, and fork left, climbing on to Melbecks Moor. The way is now eastwards to a cairn and on, past two more cairns, to a broad track going east between re-worked spoil heaps. After $1^1/_2$ miles, at Level House Bridge, cross Flincher Gill and turn right through a gate along an old miner's track – (**Gruver's Trod**),with Hard Level Gill on your right, to Old Gang Smelting Mill. Beyond the smelt mill keep on the track for a further $1^1/_2$ miles to reach the Langthwaite–Low Row road. Turn right over Surrender Bridge and take the road uphill. Opposite No. 4 grouse butt, bear right along a green track going south-west over elevated road for $^1/_2$ mile and where it turns left and downhill to Smarber, go straight ahead along a green track, first by a wall, then along the escarpment. Once through a metal gate marked 'Please Close The Gate' turn left down a winding green track for 1 mile, passing Heights, to return to Gunnerside.

POINTS OF INTEREST:

Gruver's Trod – An old miner's track to the lead mines along Gunnerside Gill. Gruvers knitted as they walked to work at 't' owd man', the miners' name for the mines. On the way they would frequently stop for a rest which they called having 'six needles'. All the mines at the head of the Gill were given girl's names.

REFRESHMENTS:

The Kings Head, Gunnerside (tel no: 0748 86261). Excellent bar meals.

Walk 44   BAINBRIDGE AND SEMER WATER   9m (14.5km)

Maps: OS Sheets Landranger 98; Outdoor Leisure 30.
Winding, walled lanes and field paths.
Start: At 935904, in Bainbridge.

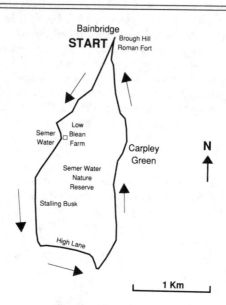

Bainbridge
START   Brough Hill
Roman Fort

Low
Semer   Blean
Water   Farm

Semer Water
Nature
Reserve

Carpley
Green

N

Stalling Busk

High Lane

1 Km

From Bainbridge (*see* Walk 38) take the A684, Aysgarth road, over the River Bain and turn right before the Stalling Busk road over a stile signposted Semer Water 2 miles. Bear left along an uphill footpath, close to a wall on your left, which dips slightly near a walled enclosure before climbing to the top of Bracken Hill. At the top Semer Water comes into view and there are lovely views of Askrigg behind and into Raydale. Ahead are two stiles. Take the signposted one on the right and follow the waymarked path through stiled fields to a high ladder stile near a gate. Go over and immediately turn right, still following waymarkers, to the River Bain. Follow the stiled path upstream to Semer Water Bridge. Cross the road and go on to the foreshore of Semer Water (*see* Walk 27), where lies the Carlow Stone (*see* Walk 27), a large limestone boulder deposited there by an ice-age glacier. Turn left along the road for $^1/_2$ mile to Low Blean Farm and turn right opposite, over a ladder stile signposted 'Stalling Busk 1 mile'. Just beyond a barn on your left, a stiled path leads close to the lake but with no access to it. Leaving the lake behind, cross two stiles into Semer Water Nature Reserve where steady climbing across a rough pasture on a good path reaches Stalling Busk's ruined church (*see* Walk 27). To continue, turn right and immediately go half left through a ruined wall where a signpost directs you up a 200ft steep climb to $^{1}/_{2}$ mile distant Stalling Busk. Now turn right, then left, to reach the Church of St Matthew, built to replace the ruined one you have just passed. Turn left by Bells Cottage, climb half-way up Butts Lane and turn right along Bob Lane. When High Lane is reached, turn right along it. Continue along this lovely green lane, from which there are some extensive views across Wensleydale and beyond, and after 2 miles turn left along Busk Lane for four most pleasant miles to return to Bainbridge, passing, at the mid way point, Carpley Green Farm from where it is all downhill. Great stuff!

REFRESHMENTS:
The Rose and Crown, Bainbridge (tel no: 0969 50225).
None *en route*.

DENT

Maps: OS Sheets Landranger 98; Outdoor Leisure 2.
A moderate walk, initially very steep, with glorious views.
Start: At 704871, the Dent car park.

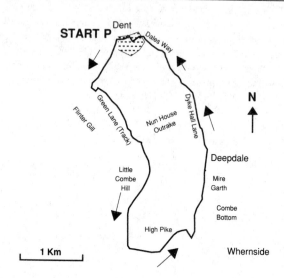

For this walk fair weather, stout shoes and a sense of humour are essential, as the Occupation Road crosses a large stretch of peat bog. From **Dent** car park cross the road, turn left for a few yards and take the first road on the right. This turns into a stony track which climbs steeply alongside Flinter Gill on to Little Combe Hill. When you reach a walled track turn left. This is the Occupation Road, an ancient drovers route, given its unusual name when the land was enclosed or 'occupied'. After 1¼ miles turn right where the road divides. Nun House Outrake, to the left, is a useful escape route back to Dent if you find the going is too boggy. The hill on your left, on the other side of Deepdale, is **Whernside**. After a further 1¾ miles the route becomes obscure and particularly boggy. As the track runs out, look half-left and you will see the walls of the track resume. On reaching a road, turn left and then take the first path on your right, signposted 'Mire Garth'. The path veers left crossing a spring, and is marked by white-topped posts. At a farm, cross a concrete path and go through the wooden gate straight ahead. Turn right through a gate alongside kennels and go through a third gate a few yards further on. Turn left and, ignoring the path to the right, continue ahead. The path crosses a spring and runs alongside Deepdale Beck for 50 yards before going off to the right. It is now marked by a series of yellow waymarks, stiles and rough footbridges across the springs flowing from Whernside.

When, after approximately 1 mile, you reach a metalled track, Dyke Hall Lane, turn left through a gate, and left again at the main road. Immediately after the road crosses the river take the path on your right, signposted 'Church Bridge'. You are now on the Dales Way which runs along first Deepdale Beck and then the River Dee. At Church Bridge the path veers left on to the main road. Continue left along the road, past the Adam Sedgwick Memorial and back to the car park.

POINTS OF INTEREST:

Dent – With its winding cobbled streets, this lovely village is well worth exploring. Although part of the Yorkshire Dales National Park, it is in fact in Cumbria. In the 17th and 18th centuries it was famous for its knitting industry, and spinning galleries can be seen on several of the houses. Dent is also famous as the birthplace of the geologist Adam Sedgwick.

Whernside – At 2415ft, this is the highest of Yorkshire's 'Three Peaks'.

Look out for a delightful series of Waterfalls running almost parallel with the Occupation Road.

REFRESHMENTS:

The Sun Inn, Dent (tel no: 058 75 208).
The Stone Close Teashop, Dent (tel no: 058 75 231).

Maps: OS Sheets Landranger 92; Outdoor Leisure 30.

A superb but strenuous traverse of moorland peat bogs and paths with glorious views.

Start: Keld.

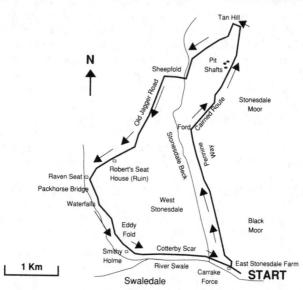

Leave Keld along a footpath signposted 'Public Footpath to Muker' at the bottom right-hand corner of the hamlet and go along the lane for 400 yards to a Pennine Way sign which directs you left down to the Swale. Cross the footbridge and go straight ahead, close to East Gill Force on your right. This is the first of several waterfalls seen on this walk. Above the waterfall, where the Pennine Way and the Coast to Coast Walks coincide, turn left along a farm track and climb up to East Stonesdale Farm. Continue along an enclosed lane on to Black Moor and keep in the same direction through gated fell pastures. The way is northward passing, on your right, Low Frith and High Frith Farms, and crossing Stonesdale Moor along a stony track. Where it ends, follow a green track to Lad Gill ford. Turn right, climbing Lad Gill Hill along a peaty path, passing fenced pitshafts to reach **Tan Hill Inn**. Here go left briefly, and left again along the Keld road for 250 yards to a sign, right, for 'Raven Seat 3 miles'. Here turn left (south-west) along a faint path, an old jagger or coal road parallel to Tan Gill, on your left. Where two sikes meet, cross the gill and continue southwards along the left bank of Stonesdale Beck, past a sheep fold, right. Just beyond where Thomas Gill enters Stonesdale Beck, cross the latter on a plank bridge and climb the south side of Thomas Gill, passing another sheepfold on your left. At the top turn left along the rim of Thomas Gill and where the track becomes faint aim for a boundary fence on higher ground and continue along it to where it turns left. Cross a corner stile with large stones on each side of it. Immediately turn left, keeping close to the fence to avoid peat bogs and when it dips go half right to ruinous **Robert's Seat House**. Continue south-west, aiming for a TV mast and descend to a way-marked stile. Cross and follow waymarked posts. Cross Hoods Bottom Beck at Jenny Whalley Force to enter the two farm hamlet of Ravenseat. Go south-east, roughly parallel to the beck on your right, following yellow markers, past cascading waterfalls and through gated pastures, edging dramatic Howe Edge and Oven Mouth Gorge. Beyond the Gorge take the lower of two paths past Vast Eddy sheepfold, left. Pass behind empty Smithy Holm Farm to reach a second farm. Beyond this go left, through a gap in a wall and eastward, crossing above Cotterby Scar, with Wain Wath Force in the Swale below. At a facing road turn left, uphill, briefly and go right along a farm road. Pass Carrake Force, below on your right, to reach East Stonesdale Farm, from where you return to Keld.

POINTS OF INTEREST:

Tan Hill Inn – England's highest at 1732ft, and famous for its sheep farms. An inscription cut into a rocky outcrop behind Tan Hill says 'In Memory of Susan Peacock, Tan Hill, who died 24 May 1937. Lived here from 1902'. She was a remarkable lady.
Robert's Seat House – Built in the 14th century for 'watchers' who protected the moors from poachers.

Maps: OS Sheets Landranger 98; Outdoor Leisure 30.
This spectacular walk is particularly well suited to all who love
solitude.
Start: At 972889, in Thornton Rust village.

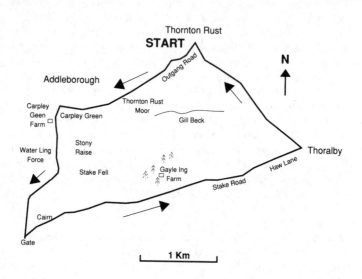

Leave Thornton Rust southwards, along a lane opposite the Village Institute. Fork left
into a walled lane, go through a gate and climb to where a bridleway sign directs you
right, along another lane, into a rough pasture. Follow the bridleway sign left, up the
rough pasture, and go through a gate in a wall. The way is now half-right across
Thornton Rust Moor, south-westwards. Beyond Gill Beck, cross a ladder stile near a
gate and continue along a ridge path, keeping to the right of Worm Gill. The tall cairn
seen over on the left is **Stony Raise**, a Bronze Age burial mound. Turn right and go
through a gate in the wall, right, and continue westwards to contour around the foot of
Addleborough on your right. Go down a pasture on your left to a corner gate and take
the path round by the wall to exit through another gate on to the **Carpley Green Road**.
    Go left, passing Carpley Green Farm on your right, and continue southwards.

Here a short detour to see lovely Water Ling Force makes a good excuse for a butty stop. The lane is subject to flooding in parts so be prepared to make slight detours or risk getting your feet wet. After 2 miles, at a signpost marked 'Bridleway Thoralby $4^1/_8$ miles', turn half-left and go towards a cairn. There fork over a pasture on an undefined route following a line of shake holes to go through a gate in a wall ahead. Continue in the same direction, between a pair of isolated gateposts, and follow a path over a long pasture, eastwards, before curving right to a double bridleway sign.

The way is now left along a gated bridle track, the Stake Road, for $1^1/_2$ miles to walled Haw Lane. Continue along this, downhill, for a further mile. The villages seen ahead are Thoralby and West Burton, with Newbiggin to your right. Where the lane bends sharply to the right, and if you don't feel like dropping into Thoralby for a pint, turn left through a corner gate and climb steeply up a track to exit through a gate at the top. Now go half-left across a pasture to a stile in the far wall and diagonally down the next field to its bottom left-hand corner where you cross Haw Beck. There is no bridge but the beck is not wide. Cross a stile and continue half-left diagonally over the next two stiled fields to Flout Moor Lane. Cross it and the stile opposite, and follow the path near a wall to drop steeply into the little valley of Gill Beck. Again there is no bridge, but although the beck is fairly wide it is shallow, and crossing is good fun. Continue uphill and over a long field and a small enclosure. Go through a gate ahead and bear right, downhill, below St Mary's Well to a stile in the far bottom corner of a wall ahead. Go half-left across the next field to exit through a signposted gate into the lane used at the start of the walk. Retrace your steps to bring to a happy conclusion an excellent, airy circular, as fine as any in Wensleydale.

POINTS OF INTEREST:

Stony Raise – A Bronze Age burial ground, supposed to contain a chest of gold known as the Golden Chest of Greenber.

Carpley Green Road – This unsurfaced road is an ancient drove road from Bainbridge in Wensleydale to Buckden in Wharfedale. The views from it as it climbs to its summit, 1758ft above sea level, are terrific and embrace Addleborough, Upper Wensleydale, Cotterdale and Wild Boar Fell.

REFRESHMENTS:

The George Inn, Thoralby (tel no: 09693 256).

Walk 48   SWINNER GILL GORGE   11m (17.5km)

Maps: OS Sheets Landranger 92 & 98; Outdoor Leisure 30.

*An easy low-level walk out, and an easy high-level return, but a
dramatically-steep central section through Swinner Gill Gorge.*

Start: At 951982, in the centre of Gunnerside.

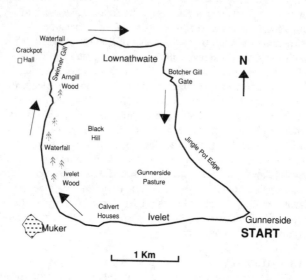

Take the more southerly of the two lanes heading west, leading quickly to the village
school and Flatlands development, through the centre of which the footpath (signposted
to Ivelet) passes. Continue through a series of gap stiles, keeping above the fence when
the path appears to be about to drop to the river, so as to climb to the top of the cliff above
it. Stay at this level, through more gap stiles and past the ubiquitous field barns, to cross
a footbridge and emerge in Ivelet. Cross the road by the telephone box and continue
climbing gently, guided by a further series of gap stiles, to Calvert Houses, where the
path goes just to the right of the first barn. Take the footpath signposted to Muker and
descend gently (more gap stiles) through a new deciduous plantation towards the river.
From hereon the path is popular, and hence well-worn. It takes you to Ramps Holme
bridge, but unless the call of the Bruce Arms at Muker is too strong to resist (it will add

another mile to the walk), do not descend to the footbridge but continue above it keeping the river on your left hand.

The dale begins to narrow under Kisdon Hill but, just before the deep gash of Swinner Gill is reached, turn right across two stiles in quick succession and climb sharply up to a grassy ledge taking you into the steeply-impressive gill. Ford the stream by the lead mine adit (which still drains the water from the deep mine workings), then leave the stream to climb the grassy bank on your left and join a footpath which becomes progressively clearer as it climbs above the crags forming the sides of the gill. The gorge itself, reached by following the beck instead of climbing above it, is passable for the slim and reasonably athletic when the water is low, but, by either route, you soon emerge at the bridge by the old lead mines. Turn right over the bridge and follow the track eastwards, climbing to cross a new road, then, following the waymark posts, reach the road a second time and turn right along it. Follow it through the gate on the watershed and continue, swinging to the right and descending, to Botcher Gill gate. The track can be followed forward to Gunnerside (*see* Walk 28), if time presses, but the hard surface provides little enjoyment and can be avoided by turning right after passing through the gate and climbing slightly to follow a watercourse over the shoulder of Silver Hill. The way soon becomes a rather indistinct footpath along the top of the scarp. Follow this past the shake holes to join a clear hollow way on Jingle Pot Edge. The descent is straight down the nose of the ridge, heading directly for Gunnerside, visible below. Enter the village over the cattle grid at its western end.

POINTS OF INTEREST:
The huge open common you have just crossed is the village cow pasture, where Gunnerside tenants' cattle have shared the grazing for many centuries. It stands in total contrast to the tiny enclosed fields traversed earlier, where they grew oats and mowed their hay, the latter being stored in the numerous field barns.

REFRESHMENTS:
The Kings Head, Gunnerside (tel no: 0748 86261).

Maps: OS Sheets Landranger 92 & 98; Outdoor Leisure 30.
Strenuous walking across moors, bogs, rough grass and heather.
Start: The Literary Institute, Gunnerside.

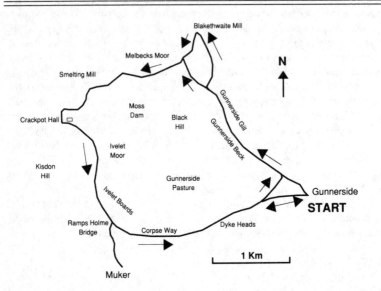

Leave Gunnerside (*see* Walk 28) along a path between South View and Rose Cottage, crossing a stile and going north-west. Climb a steep grassy bank dotted with hawthorn bushes and pockmarked with shake holes to a broad, stony bridleway. Climb steadily along the western side of Gunnerside Hill passing, far below, the ruined remains of Sir Francis Mine and, further on, Bunton Level. After $1^{1}/_{2}$ miles go through a wooden gate and cross Botcher Gill. Beyond there is a choice of routes. The shorter one follows a sandy track leftwards and uphill for 1 mile to High Whim to rejoin the main route. The longer, main route is great walking for stronger hikers. Its way is right along a narrow, boggy track which broadens to a close-cropped, grassy track leading downhill through heather for 1 mile to the impressive remains of **Blakethwaite Mill** at the top end of Gunnerside Gill. From the Mill go up along a slanting path, to the left of Blind Gill, which zig-zags steeply to just above North Hush where the shorter route welcomes it back. Go westwards on a broad track that climbs gradually across open **Melbecks Moor** for 1 mile passing, just beyond a wooden gate, the walk's highest point, 1895ft above sea level.

Continue along the track to where a white painted signpost points left down the right-hand side of Grain Gill. Take this boggy, downhill path, which is well waymarked with yellow posts, to Swinner Hill with its waterfalls and the ruined Smelting Mill (1770–1821). The way down to the miners' bridge over the beck is as rough as some of the walkers using it. A detour in the form of a rough scramble upstream from the bridge will bring you to a 70ft cave hidden by a waterfall. In the 17th century this cave was used by Swaledale folk as a secret place of worship and so came to be called Swinner Gill Kirk. Return to the bridge, cross it and go right up a track to a gate at the top, from which the views down Swaledale are superb. Take the track downhill, passing between an empty smithy on the right and Crackpot Hall ruins on the left, once the highest inhabited farm in England. Go down to a lane. Turn left down a gated track and go over Swinner Gill. Continue along a well used track along level riverside fields for $1^1/_2$ miles to Ramps Holme Bridge. Here the views of Kisdon and the River Swale's gorge are most spectacular. At Ramps Holme Bridge an easy path will bring you to the lovely village of Muker which has tearooms and a pub. It makes a most pleasant detour. Back at Ramps Holme Bridge re-cross it and continue down stream to join the Corpse Way, a medieval funeral route from Keld to Grinton. Here a double signpost points you eastward along a path which soon becomes an elevated road which will take you back to Gunnerside.

POINTS OF INTEREST:

Blakethwaite Mill – With its hillside flue, peat house and single slab bridge was opened in 1821 and operated until 1878.

Melbecks Moor – The extensive views from the summit embrace Buckden Pike, Great Whernside, Lovely Seat, Great Shunner Fell and the twin reservoirs of Moss Dam.

REFRESHMENTS:

The King's Head, Gunnerside (tel no: 0748 86261).
The Farmer's Arms, Muker (tel no: 0748 86297).
Muker Tea Shop: The Old School Craft Shop/Tea Room, Muker (tel no: 0748 86409

Walk 50   CASTLE BOLTON   11m (18km)

Maps: OS Sheets Landranger 98; Outdoor Leisure 30.

This is a grand mix of high and low level walking, offering panoramic views.

Start: The car park in Castle Bolton.

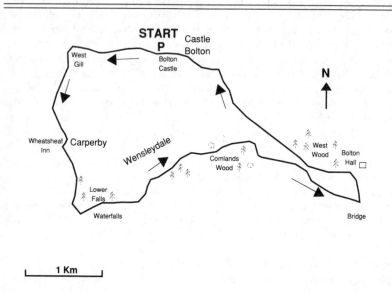

From the car park go right over a stile signposted 'Aysgarth 3 miles' and then westwards along an unsurfaced track through fields. After 1½ miles ford West Gill and go left through a gate signposted 'Carperby'. Continue along a path across a rough pasture with a scattering of hawthorns and through another signposted gateway. Continue downhill and at the triple signpost go left for ½ mile into Carperby (*see* Walk 42). Turn right into the village and opposite the Wheatsheaf Inn go through a gate, then left, southwards, to Low Lane. Cross to a stile, beyond which you follow a clear path through stiled fields into Freeholders Wood. Now bear right, downhill, to the Carperby road. Turn left and go under a railway bridge, then past Aysgarth car park and Information Centre on your right to reach the River Ure. Before crossing it, leave the road and detour upstream for a close inspection of the Upper Falls, clearly seen ahead.

Back at the road, cross Yore Bridge and climb the steps ahead beside the museum to St Andrew's Church, which is well worth a visit. Go in front of it and eastwards through the churchyard to cross a stile into a field. Cross the field to another stile. Cross and continue with the river close to you on your left passing the Middle Falls then the Lower Falls. Keep in the same direction along a clear path to the entrance to Hestholme Farm on the A684. Go left, crossing Bishopdale Beck on Hestholme Farm Bridge. Take the first stile on your left and follow the path eastwards, beside the river. At Wellclose Plantation climb the steep path away from the riverside and, at the top of the hill, cross a signposted stile. Turn left and follow yellow marker posts to the top of the field. Turn right along an elevated, stiled path. Continue eastward over four more fields to enter Comlands Wood over a ladder stile and descend a stepped path to Red Mere Force. Follow the signs out of the wood, then go left along a field and over another ladder stile. Continue eastwards over fields following an intermittent track.

When High Wanlass Farm is seen on your right, join a gated riverside path to a stream with a triple signpost, where you go eastward across some stiled fields to a tree lined lane. Go left, down the lane, and cross the River Ure on Ford's Bridge. Now take the drive through Bolton Hall Park and, as you approach the Hall, go through a gate, then left, along a track edging West Wood for a mile and out through a kissing gate. Now cross a series of stiled pastures for 1 mile to reach Redmere along Well Lane. Go right, up the village, and opposite Hogra Farm, go left by the village hall. Pass the Bolton Arms and beyond the school, go under the railway bridge, then left at the footpath sign and follow a path parallel to the line serving Redmine Quarry. Where the railway ends, continue across stiled pastures to enter **Castle Bolton**, the end of an excellent walk.

POINTS OF INTEREST:
Castle Bolton – The castle, where Mary Queen of Scots was kept prisoner, is well worth a visit. St Oswald's Church across the road from the castle, also warrants a visit.

REFRESHMENTS:
The Bolton Arms, Castle Bolton (tel no: 0969 23327).

Walk 51   **HAWES AND TEN END**   13m (20km)

Maps: OS Sheets Landranger 98; Outdoor Leisure 30 & 31.

A strenuous walk, in the steps of the drovers. One demanding climb.

Start: The car park in Gayle Lane at the west end of Hawes.

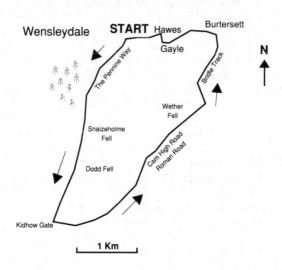

Leave the car park going up Gayle Lane to a stile signposted 'Mossy Lane' opposite Wensleydale Creameries and take the path across five stiled fields to Mossy Lane. Continue westwards across two more fields to the B6255 and go left along it for about 150 yards. Where it bends right go left along an old drove road called West Cam Road. It is a tough, uphill slog but you will be rewarded with magnificent all round views. At the top, where you cross a ladder stile beside a gate, have a breather and enjoy what's on offer. The going is easier now, south-west along an open fell track over Backsides, until, just past Snaizholme Plantation, on your right, the stone track climbs steeply, giving you some fine views of Ingleborough. The Pennine Way joins West Cam Road 2 miles from the B6255, meeting it obliquely from the left. A cairn displaying the words 'Cam Road–Pennine Way Hawes' in white acknowledges this marriage of routes.

Anyone wishing to shorten the walk can do so here by turning left and taking the Pennine Way down the cairned flank of Ten End to **Gayle** and on to Hawes. The way ahead continues along a high level green lane for a further 2$^{1}/_{2}$ miles along the side of Dodd Fell to the junction of West Cam Road and Cam High Road. At that point there is a signpost showing 'Horton 8 miles–Hawes 5 miles'. From here the Three Peaks – Whernside, Ingleborough and Pen-y-Ghent, backed by Fountains Fell – look magnificent. Turn left, leaving the Pennine Way, along Cam High Road for 2$^{1}/_{2}$ miles to join the Hawes–Kettlewell Road and continue along it for $^{1}/_{2}$ mile to where, just before the road descends, you go right along walled Cam High Road for 2 miles across the side of Drumaldrace and Wether Fell. At a signpost 'Gayle 1$^{1}/_{2}$ miles' cross a wall stile on your left and go straight ahead, over the brow of the fell, on a curving path, downhill to a facing stone wall with no stile. Climb over the wall and continue along a clear path, through a gateway near a hut. Keep on this meandering track for 2 miles to Burtersett. Once in the hamlet turn right in front of Meadow Cottage, turn left, down the street, passing, on your right, Hillway Hall. Turn left just beyond the Methodist Chapel and take the path through a gated stile and across fields to Hawes. The way is paved with sandstone flags and is easy to follow. It brings you, via Old Gayle Lane to the A684 just beyond the Wensleydale Press. Turn left along the A684 into Hawes carrying an armful of happy memories.

POINTS OF INTEREST:

Gayle – Hillary Hall, was built in 1729 and named after the same Hillary family whose famous descendant Edmund Hilary was one of the conquerors of Everest.

Walking westerly across the fields to Mossy Lane the view northwards includes Great Shunner Fell (2340ft), Lovely Seat (2213ft), Hugh Seat (2257ft) and High Seat (2328ft). The retrospective view takes in Addleborough (1864ft) and Wether Fell (2105ft). From the top of the stiff climb up West Cam Road unfolding views reveal Hawes and Hardraw with, further back, Cotterdale, Wild Boar Fell and Baugh (pronounced 'Bo') Fell. From Cam High Road there are good views into Wharfedale with Buckden Pike prominent.

REFRESHMENTS:

Numerous in Hawes.

Walk 52   **HAWES AND COTTERDALE**   14m (22.5km)
Maps: OS Sheets Landranger 98; Pathfinder SD 88/98 & 89/99.
Map and compass needed. Do not attempt in doubtful weather.
Start: At 876898, in Hawes.

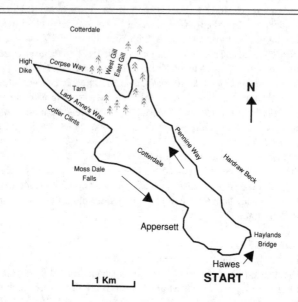

Leave Hawes along Brunt Acres Road and at the entrance to Hawes Rural Workshops
cross the signposted stile and take the flagged path across two fields to rejoin the road.
Turn left, cross Haylands Bridge and after 150m turn left across a stepped stile and
follow a paved path to Hardraw. Turn left across the bridge and, beyond the old school,
turn right at a Pennine Way sign and take a lane, climbing steeply, to reach open fell
over a ladder stile. Continue along a green track, climbing steadily for a mile to cross
another ladder stile where the track climbs Hearne Top. Just beyond it, at a bridleway
signpost, turn left, away from the Pennine Way and follow a track high above
Cotterdale. At an unsignposted gate, left, enter South Wood and meander downhill
along a broad drive. On the straight stretch near the valley bottom look for an easily
missed path, right, leading to a footbridge over East Gill. Cross and follow a clear track
into Cotterdale. Just before a cottage with a bellcote, take the signposted stile, right, and

continue through gated fields with West Gill on your left. In the third field cross a stile where the fence on your left meets a wall. Go over West Gill and take the thin track bearing right into Cotterdale Forest. The track bends left, up a very steep side of the valley, crossing an unsurfaced road. At the top, at the edge of the forest, cross a stile and continue across open moor, climbing more gradually. Aim for the right-hand corner of a fence which comes into view on the horizon. From the fence corner go west on a clear track, following marker posts to ruined **High Dike Farm.** Turn left along a green packhorse route for 2 miles. When the track descends below a lime kiln go through the smaller of two gates in the wall ahead and descend to a stile over the wall on your right. Go half-right over a pasture towards the far side of a wood. Cross a stile and go diagonally down a pathless pasture to a stile into a wood. Take the sloping track through the wood, cross the River Ure ahead, go over the A684 and climb a signposted stile. Go uphill close to a wall, left, over the brow of the hill and half right across a field to a stile in its bottom corner. Turn left through a waymarked gateway and cross a bridge over Mossdale Gill. Following waymarkers, go left between Mossdale Head Farm buildings and down Mossdale Beck to the River Ure. Go forward and climb a rusty gate in a hedge ahead. Go along a track in the next field. The track becomes a broad footpath: follow it for 1 mile past Birkrigg Farm and leave it at a triple footpath sign, turning right, through valley bottom fields and up a wooded hillside. Turn left and follow stiled pastures for a mile to rejoin the River Ure for a riverside walk to New Bridge. Follow a field path alongside the road to Appersett. Cross the bridge over Widdale Beck and turn right along a lane, climbing steadily. Go under Appersett Viaduct and immediately turn left. Go half-right across the adjacent field, cross a ladder stile and cross the next field to a gate in the far wall. Turn left along the field's edge to cross a stile near the corner. Turn half-left aiming for a gate in a wall ahead and go down a track to the A684 near Ashes. A short walk along it will bring you back into Hawes.

POINTS OF INTEREST:
High Dike Farm – Once an inn popular with packmen. The highwayman Swift Nick frequently stayed there when the heat was on further south.

REFRESHMENTS:
There are a lot of pubs and cafés in Hawes.
The Green Dragon, Hardraw (tel no: 09697 392).

Walk 53   ILKLEY   3m (5km)

Maps: OS Sheets Landranger 104; Pathfinder SE 04/14.
A short, moderately easy walk, steep in places, visiting an 18th century bathhouse and a beautiful wooded ravine.
Start: At 118477, Ilkley Station.

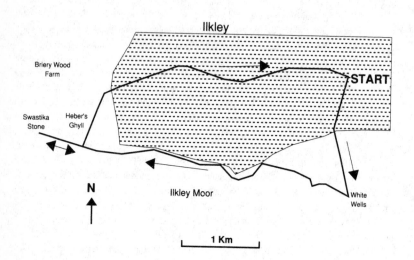

From **Ilkley** station, cross the main road, go a few yards to your right and turn left up Wells Road. Immediately after the cattle grid bear slightly left on to Ilkley Moor and take the path leading to **White Wells**, the whitewashed cottage on the hillside. Leave the cottage via the metalled path, to the left as you face the town. Just beyond some railings, after the path loops round to the right, take the grassy path on the left. At the road turn left for a few yards, and then take the path to your right which runs alongside an old wall. As you reach a small reservoir on your right, the view suddenly opens up, giving a wonderful panorama of the Dales. Follow the path over a footbridge and, after passing through a small gap in a wall, make for the semi-circle of railings ahead. These protect the mysterious **Swastika Stone**: the view from here is particularly good.

Retrace your steps to just before the footbridge and go through the gate on your left. This path will take you down the idyllic Heber's Ghyll via a series of rustic bridges which criss-cross the stream. When you reach the road, turn right and follow Grove Road back to the town centre. What could be a tedious stretch of road walking is amply compensated for by some magnificent Victorian and Edwardian architecture, bearing witness to Ilkley's wealthy past. **Heathcote**, on the left, designed by Sir Edwin Lutyens in 1906, is particularly fine. At the end of Grove Road, turn right to return to the station.

POINTS OF INTEREST:

Ilkley – A historic town, the site of the Roman fortress of *Olicana*. In the 19th century it became a fashionable and prosperous spa. Ilkley Moor is a dramatic backdrop to the town and must be the most famous area of countryside in Britain. It is common land, so visitors are free to wander across it at will.

White Wells – Built in the mid 18th century to capture the spa waters flowing from the moor. Infirm visitors would bathe in the icy water in a stone bath! The cottage is open to the public and has a tearoom.

The Swastika Stone – Thought to be Bronze Age: One of many carved stones on the moor. The symbol, signifying eternal life, has also been found in Europe and India.

REFRESHMENTS:

The Rose and Crown, Church Street, Ilkley (tel no: 0943 607260).
Betty's, Church Street, Ilkley (tel no: 0943 608029).

Maps: OS Sheets Landranger 98; Outdoor Leisure 10.

A short, easy walk, steep in places, to two waterfalls and a historic packhorse bridge.

Start: At 821674, the car park at Stainforth, just off the B6479.

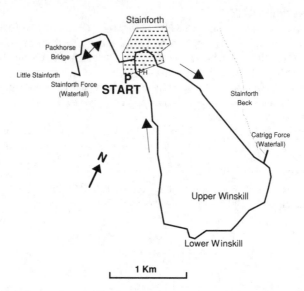

From **Stainforth**, turn right out of the car park and left along the road signposted 'Halton Gill'. Go over the green on your right, cross Stainforth Beck via the stepping stones, then bear left up a stony lane. At the top of this lane go left down a steep hill to Catrigg Force. Take care as the hill can be slippery when it is wet and you come upon the force very suddenly.

Return to the lane. The views from here are splendid with Pen-y-Ghent ahead of you as you face Catrigg, and Fountains Fell to the right. Go over the stile at the end of the lane and turn left. Cross a further stile and follow the signpost to Winskill. When your path is crossed by another path, go through the gate marked Lower Winskill and down the lane. Pass the house and go through a yard to cross a ladder stile. Follow the path, right, alongside the wall to cross a further stile and then go half left (the path is

112

obscure here) over an area of exposed limestone. A further stile takes you into a small copse and then passes alongside a limestone scar. At the end of the scar go through the gap in the wall and take the leftmost fork of the path down to the road. Turn right over the bridge, left past the car park and right at the main road.

Take the first turning on the left over the railway bridge to reach the beautiful **Packhorse Bridge** at Little Stainforth. Just over the bridge a footpath to your left takes you to Stainforth Falls, idyllically set on a bend in the River Ribble. After visiting the falls, trace your steps to the car park.

POINTS OF INTEREST:

Stainforth – Derives its name from the 'stony ford' which linked the two settlements – Stainforth and Little Stainforth – on either side of the River Ribble. Once on an important packhorse route between York and Lancaster.

The Packhorse Bridge – At Little Stainforth is now owned by the National Trust. It was built in the 1670s.

REFRESHMENTS:

The Craven Heifer, Stainforth (tel no: 07292 2599).

Walk 55   TARN MOOR CIRCULAR $3\frac{1}{2}$m (5.6km)

Maps: OS Sheets Landranger 103; Outdoor Leisure 10.

A pleasant circular walk through Civil War country.

Start: Skipton Parish Church.

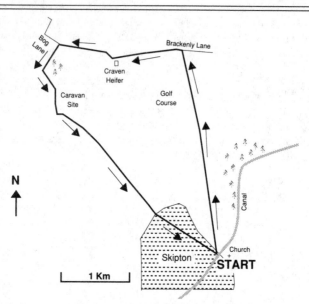

From Skipton Parish Church go right, along the Grassington road, passing the Castle Inn, crossing the canal and turning right up Chapel Hill. Where the road bifurcates, take the left fork, going uphill to enter a field over a stile beside a gate. Continue northwards up the field to exit over another stile beside a gate at the top. From this vantage point the views of Skipton and the Aire valley are excellent. Continue along the footpath ahead, going down hill to reach the busy Skipton by-pass road. Cross the by-pass to a stile and go over into a field to the left of a golf course. Keeping in the same direction, cross the field to a stile on the brow of the hill ahead. Cross to reach the golf course. Continue straight ahead to the corner of two stone walls. There go over a stone stile and on to a gate. Go through into a field. Cross the field, keeping close to its left-hand side, to reach another stile. Cross to reach Brackenly Lane to the north of Tarn Moor. Turn left, along it, to reach the main road from Skipton to Grassington. To the left of the

T-junction stands the Craven Heifer Inn, which makes a handy mid-walk refreshment stop.

From the T-junction cross the road to the stile immediately opposite and go over to a field. Cross the field and exit at a stile opposite. Continue over the next field, aiming for an electricity pole, and keep in the same direction to reach a stile beside a gate. Cross to reach Bog Lane. Turn left along it. About 100 yards after passing Tarn House Farm, go over a large stile on your left into a field. Cross the field, going between two large trees to an old kissing gate. Go through into a lane. Now turn right and follow waymarkers around the right side of a caravan park. When a wooden stile is reached, cross it to enter a large field. Continue ahead, passing an electricity pole, to a tree on the horizon and, keeping it on your right, continue in the same direction to cross a broken stile on to a busy road. Cross the road and the stile immediately opposite into a field. Cross the road to reach the Skipton to Stirton road over another stile. Turn left along it and on reaching Skipton go down hill along Raikes Road until Skipton Parish Church, the end of a grand little walk, is reached.

POINTS OF INTEREST:
The earthworks you cross on hill approaching the by-pass were thrown up during the Civil War when there was much local action.
Arum lilies, violets, wood sorrel and many other plants grow in the hedgerow along Bog Lane.

REFRESHMENTS:
Hotels, pubs and cafés in Skipton.
The Craven Heifer Inn (tel no: 0756 792521).

Walk 56   EMBSAY CRAG   3½m (5.5km)

Maps: OS Sheets Landranger 103 & 104; Outdoor Leisure 10.
A gradual climb up a heather-topped hill to Embsay Crag, a
scramble over the rocks and a steep descent to the reservoir.
Start: At 009538, the car park on Main Street, Embsay.

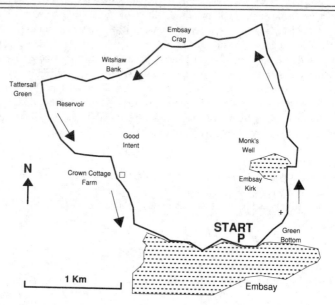

Cross the stile at the back of the car park in **Embsay** and go half-right
across the field. Cross two further stiles to reach the road. Follow the road left, past
the church, and 70 yards after the road bends sharply to the right, take the metalled path
on your left, signposted 'Bridleway Embsay Crag and Reservoir'. Take this path past
the farm and over a stile on to a track. Follow the track, which passes through two gates,
to open moorland. Note: these gates are across the track, not the ones to the right. A few
yards after the second gate the path forks half-left to the top of the hill and Embsay Crag.

    Once you have scrambled down the rocks of the crag take the path which leads to
the right-hand side of the reservoir. At the gate, turn left and follow this quiet, walled
road towards Embsay. After 1 mile, when you see some ponds on your right, follow the
path on your left, which will take you back to the car park.

POINTS OF INTEREST:
Embsay – Has some lovely old buildings, but its main attraction is a 2 mile steam railway which aims to take visitors back to the age of branchline steam (tel no: 0756 794727 for timetable).

REFRESHMENTS:
The Elm Tree Inn, Embsay (tel no: 0756 790717).

Maps: OS Sheets Landranger 104; Pathfinder SE 03/13.
A short walk in Brontë Land.
Start: The car park near the church, Haworth.

Walk to the church and turn left into the churchyard with the railings on the left and graves on the right. Keep ahead with metal railings on both sides, and pass through a gate on to an old paved path along which the Brontë family walked on their way to the moor. Follow the path to the first turning on the right and go up this narrow lane to a minor road. Cross and take the path on the left, up through the heather, aiming for the corner of a hill, keeping right of the 4th pylon. The track bears slightly right and goes to the point at the top of the hill. Go right for 25 yards. From here you can see Lower Laithe reservoir and, 4 miles away over the moor, left of the reservoir, another moor. There on the skyline is the farm Wuthering Heights.

Now turn left along the track, going between the reservoir and the pylons. After 300 yards it joins a cart-track and 50 yards further on comes to a crossing of cart-tracks with a quarry on the left. Take the first track on the right and follow it until it swings left in a half circle. Walk forward bearing left and passing down a rough part of the track with a small quarry on the left. Now go up and down three times to walk towards an old farm under a tree on the edge of the moor and fields. The track now joins three moor cart-tracks, with a white farmhouse in front. Take the track in front bearing left to a minor road. Turn left, then right off the road up the lane to Upper Westfield farm under the tree. Pass the farm and go over the stile next to the gate. Turn left down the field, passing a wood on your left, and go through a farm gate, keeping left of Westfield Farm and Leeshaw Reservoir. At the bottom of the lane, turn left at the back of a farm and follow the lane to the crossroads. Turn right down Moorside Lane. After 150yds turn left to Pin Hill End Farm. The narrow track passes along a double walled ginnel in front of the farm. Next go over a stone stile to a farm with three stiles. Take the left one, and pass a beautiful house built in 1742. At the end of the house bear left through a ginnel in front of some cottages and pass through a metal gate to an old paved path. Go over a stile into a lane and turn right. Bear left behind cottages and go over a gap stile. Go along Moorhouse Lane to a road at a letter box and turn left to a junction. Turn right along Marsh Lane, then left up Old Oxenhope Lane to the first bend. There turn right beyond the farm and go over a gap stile. Turn left along the right side of the wall and go through a gap stile to a paved path. At the top of the field pass into a narrow lane along the bottom of a field with a wall on the right and cross a green double lane. Go over stiles, descending gently to a farm. Here bear left up a double walled road with the farm on the right. At the first bend go over a stile and across two fields to reach a stile. Go over and turn right down the ginnel. Go left with the path, then right and left again. Now the ginnel widens and the path joins the outward path. Retrace your steps to the start of the walk.

POINTS OF INTEREST:

Haworth – A village best visited during the week. There are enough Brontë sites to keep the enthusiast happy for many an hour, while even those who have not read the book will be fascinated by the family home.

REFRESHMENTS:

There are lots of tempting tea shops in Haworth village.

Walk 58   NUMBERSTONES END   5m (8km)

Maps: OS Sheets Landranger 98; Outdoor Leisure 10.
A steep climb for a superb view of Wharfedale, but an easy return through level pastures.
Start: At 032612, Burnsall village.

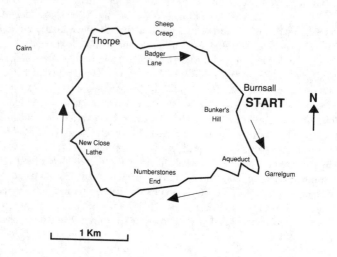

N.B. The Barden Moor Access Agreement allows no dogs.

Numberstones End is the steep crag above the village, up which a fell race is held each summer. The route described here is a much easier one, starting along the Bolton Abbey road past the Fell Hotel, but leaving it 500 yards further on where the plantation begins. The steep track on the right through the woods provides access to Barden Moor, on which there are few public rights of way though an Access Agreement allows the public to wander freely, unless shooting is in progress. The track takes you to the south corner of the wood, where you cross a stile to reach the moor. Turn back right, along the wall, until, on arriving at the far corner of the wood, you can look down on Burnsall. Turn back now, to the south, climbing steeply on a good green track. On reaching a little plateau, turn right through the bracken to reach a rocky gully, from which you emerge

120

to find an extensive view over Wharfedale. The track continues as a **Hollow Way** curving round the northern shoulder of the hill.

When the way becomes indistinct, continue forward to join a fell-runner's track from Burnsall. Turn left and follow it to a ridge leading to the prominent cairn ahead. This splendid viewpoint is not the summit, so continue along a narrow but distinct track which hugs the top of the steep slopes falling to your right. Arriving at another cairn – the real summit of Numberstones End – make for the shooting box ahead (due west), either by taking a straight line through the heather, or by turning south-west to join a wide sandy track which takes you to the same place. At the shooting box, leave the main track by turning right along a smaller one at right-angles which passes a filled-in coal pit and then starts to descend, becoming a deep hollow way as it does so. Follow it, with many changes in direction to avoid the most difficult ground, past a cairn and a disused stone quarry, to the moor wall, from which point the name Thorpe-in-the-Hollow, sometimes given to the village below, is seen to be most appropriate. Go through the gate into the walled lane, and follow it down into the village. Fork right at the bottom and follow the lane up to the brow of the hill. There fork right again, along the walled green lane signposted to Burnsall. Where the lane ends, turn right over the stile then go down to the gate below. On passing through it, veer left to reach the stile in the bottom corner of the field. Cross the plank bridge and go up the field beyond, keeping the barn well to your right. Pass through two gap stiles in succession to reach Badger Lane, which you cross at right angles and go straight on. Burnsall now appears in view ahead, and is reached by crossing a number of well-built stone stiles. On emerging, through a yard, into the main street, turn right to return to Burnsall bridge and green.

POINTS OF INTEREST:
Hollow Way – Hollow ways were made by the carriage of peat or of coal down from the moor, using packhorses or sledges.

REFRESHMENTS:
The Red Lion Inn (tel no: 075672 204).
The Fell Hotel (tel no: 075672 209).

Walk 59   **BRADFIELD**   5m (8km)

Maps: OS Sheets Landranger 110; Pathfinder SK 29/39.

Beautiful, even though it is always in sight of Sheffield.

Start: The stream–side car park off The Sands, Low Bradfield.

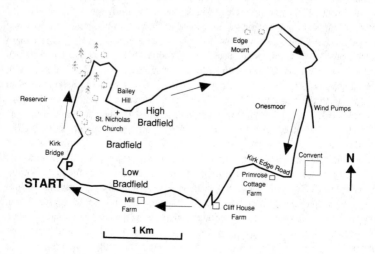

Walk along The Sands to reach the stream. Turn left and cross the second footbridge. Go up steps to a road, turn left and walk by the side of Agden Reservoir. Just before the corner of the reservoir a stone gateway with a step stile is reached on the right. Take the track uphill into the wood. Reach the edge of the wood and turn right down the track by the wood side. This can be wet. Cross a stream and re-enter the wood through a kissing gate. The path goes uphill along a wallside, through a gateway, and along the steep, wooded side of Bailey Hill. Emerge from the wood, cross a stile and pass through gates to reach **St Nicholas Church** in **High Bradfield**. Turn right, in front of the church and left along its side to reach a metal gateway. Go through and turn left along Jane Street.

    Cross the road reached and go over the stile by a gateway. Walk uphill along the stream side, bearing right to a gateway. Follow the wall side to another gateway and cross the field to go over a stile in a wall corner. Bear right, still going uphill, and along the wall side. Bear left to a stone stile a few yards from a gate. Cross the road and climb over a second stone stile. Bear left by the side of small quarry holes and go along a faint grass track. To the left of a building, a wooden stile is the first of a series crossed while bearing left across the small fields to reach a wall corner by trees. Cross the stile and turn right, along the road, to a crossroads. Turn right towards Low Bradfield, reaching a ladder stile and footpath sign on the right. Cross a field bearing slightly left to reach a stone stile a few yards to the right of two gateways. Go over and cross the large field, aiming a little to the right of the buildings of the convent to reach a wall by its side. Follow this to a road and turn right.

A footpath sign on the left helps find a less distinct stone stile. Bear right, downhill, and go through the left-hand gateway. Take the track downhill to Cliffe House Farm. Pass through the gateway and turn right along the surfaced track. Reach a wooden chalet and turn left to cross the stile by the gate side. Follow the tarmacked path beyond down to a road and cross to the right to reach a ladder stile. Beyond, descend steadily, with views of Damflask reservoir below. Bear right to a gateway and cross a field to a stone stile in the opposite corner. Turn left through a gateway and right along the wall side down to a gap and then a ladder stile. Cross to the far right-hand corner to a stone stile. Go ahead to a wooden stile, then down steps to bear a little left to reach a ladder stile. Descend slightly to a gap in the wall, bear left to the wall corner and go through a squeeze stile. Go over a stone stile, and follow the wallside over more stiles to the right of Mill Farm. Follow the track reached down to the road back into **Low Bradfield**.

POINTS OF INTEREST:
St Nicholas Church – A 15th century building. The gatehouse was built in the 18th century to help guard against body snatchers. Church keys are kept at the gatehouse. **Bradfield** – A village of two parts, High and Low. The nearby reservoirs supply Sheffield.

REFRESHMENTS:
The Old Horns Inn, High Bradfield (tel no: 0742 81207).

Walks 60 & 61   **RIVELIN VALLEY**   5m (8km) or 9m (14.5km)
Maps: OS Sheets Landranger 110; Pathfinder SK 28/38.
A moderately hilly walk on the edge of Sheffield. Some agility helps.
Start: The car park by the bank of the River Rivelin near the junction of the A57 and the A6101.

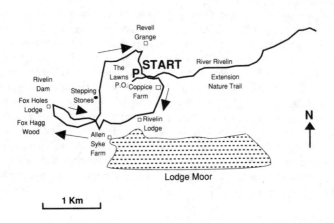

Cross the road and look at the Rivelin Nature Trail notice board. Walk a few yards along the riverside and cross the bridge. The bridleway quickly turns uphill to the A57. Cross and go up the driveway of Blackbrook Farm (on the map this is Coppice Farm). Cross a stile and walk along the narrow path uphill through Blackbrook Wood. Keep the brook close below on the left ignoring paths to the right. Reach a junction with stepping stones across the brook. Do not cross but turn right uphill to the wall corner. Walk by the wall side to reach a road near Rivelin Lodge. The views are excellent here. Cross the road and descend a little to the right before turning left along a footpath. Keep to the path which contours along the hillside. Do not descend along the wider track or ascend the footpath soon reached on the left. The path bears left as it descends a little

124

to reach Allen Syke: cross the stream and turn right. Bear left to reach a junction of paths. Note the path downhill through the trees. Bear left uphill along a very narrow path which goes above the steep, tree-covered hillside. Rivelin Dam is below, and just before drawing level with it, you will reach a path descending to the woodland below. The path is not always clear, so look out for guide posts and dots of yellow paint. There are a few steps, and the path bears a little to the right just before passing to the left of a holly bush. Fox Holes Lodge is reached near the corner of the dam.

You may wish to walk a little way along the road by the side of the dam before continuing along the footpath which bears right and gently uphill before the wall and the road. Keep to the wider, clearer track through Fox Hagg Wood where small streams need careful crossing to avoid the mud. Branches on the ground and on the trees help. The path junction noted earlier is reached again. Turn left down the narrow, but clear, path to the left of Allen Syke. Concrete stepping stones ensure safe crossing of the Rivelin, and an enclosed path leads up to the A57. Cross and go through the stile opposite. Cross the field to the gateway in the centre of a wall ahead and maintain direction uphill to a wall corner, across a farm track, and to a stile below Rivelin Rocks. Cross and take the path right. Pass a junction and continue with a wall on your right. Reach a lane and cross a stile down through a field to a stile and another lane below. Turn left to the road and turn right downhill to cross the A6101 and reach the car park.

The walk can be extended by following the nature trail which itself follows the Rivelin for 2 miles almost to the centre of Sheffield and has much of industrial archaeological interest, including water wheels. A guide can be obtained from museums and libraries, and Rivelin Post Office.

REFRESHMENTS:
None *en route*, though there are plenty nearby in Sheffield.

Walk 62 FROM WHIRLOW PARK TO THE OX STONES 5m (8km)

Maps: OS Sheets Landranger 110; Pathfinder SK 28/38.

A delightful woodland and moorland walk close to Sheffield.

Start: The main car park, Whirlow Brook Park.

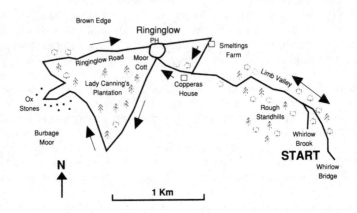

The well-signed woodland path joins a broad track into the Limb Valley. Go through woodland for $1\frac{1}{2}$ miles to the hamlet of Ringinglow using a stone causeway over east field. A stile gives access to Sheephill Road. After 100 yards, where the road bends go down Houndkirk track, an ancient turnpike route. After nearly a mile the track meets another known as the Jumble Road. Turn right here at the corner of Lady Canning's Plantation. For a further $\frac{1}{2}$ mile you fringe the woodland copse and then strike out left across the moorland slope to the windswept heights of the silhouetted gritstone blocks known as the Ox Stones. These rugged monoliths are likened to the shape of fat oxen and command a lofty view point along the ridge of Burbage Moor. From around 1300ft the whole of South Yorkshire spreads before you like an aerial map. Retrace your steps to the trig point. This moorland area was once a grouse-shooting area owned by the Duke of Rutland. Today it is still blackened after a disastrous fire of 1976 which was started carelessly in the nearby plantation destroying 4 square miles of moorland. Rejoin the track by the side of the wood and head left to the upper reaches of the Ringinglow Road. This highway splits the region of the Burbage and Hallam Moors and is a popular route for motorists travelling to the Hope Valley and the rock climbing grounds of Stanage Edge. Walk right for $^1/_2$ mile to the hamlet of Ringinglow. Keep forward in the direction of Bents Green and Ecclesall for $^1/_4$ mile to a footpath sign pointing right at Smeltings Farm. Go over three fields and stiles to rejoin the Limb Valley track at the ruined **Copperas House**. Retrace the outward route to the start.

POINTS OF INTEREST:
Copperas House – Lead was smelted here in the 18th century.

REFRESHMENTS:
The Shepley Spitfire Hotel, Mickley Lane, Totley (tel no: 0742 360298). bar meals etc.
The Old Mother Redcap Inn, Prospect Road, Bradway (tel no: 0742 360179). Bar meals.
The Norfolk Arms Inn, Ringinglow Road (tel no: 0742 302197). An old coaching inn. Bar meals etc.
The Whirlow Brook Park Hall (tel no: 0742 759852). Full catering facilities and café.
The Beauchief Hotel, Abbeydale Road South (tel no: 0742 620500). A three star hotel, high class accommodation, facilities.
The Castle Inn, 20 Well Lane, Bradway (tel no: 0742 362955). Bar meals.
The Rising Sun Hotel, Abbey Lane (tel no: 0742 360778). Full meals. High class.

Walk 63   THE BLACKA MOOR CIRCUIT   5¹⁄₂m (9km)

Maps: OS Sheets Landranger 110; Pathfinder SK 28/38.

A moorland and woodland walk across the lovely Blacka Moor.

Start: Totley Bus Terminus.

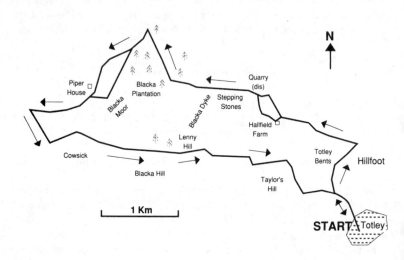

From the bus terminus go right down Hillfoot Road. After 150 yards turn left at a bend in the road into Chapel Lane, a cobbled causeway. Go across the field to Penny Lane. Turn left for 200 yards past the quaint, old-fashioned Cricket Inn and a sports field. Enter Bents Farm over a stile by a fingerpost and cross two fields. Bear left to the backwater hamlet of Old Hay. Cross the footbridge over Old Hay Brook and proceed along a drive to the left of Avenue Farm. Notice the weir across the field. Yellow markers direct you to the top of the drive. Cross two fields going gently upwards to reach Shorts Lane (home of the popular Dore Riding Stables). Join a bridleway to the left. From here you can see **Blacka Moor** ahead. There is a fingerpost and notice board at the entrance to the woodland. Pass Blacka Dyke stream on the left while going along the main Piper House Gate route. Go over a ford, and 50 yards further on cross a tiny footbridge where a fingerpost points right through mixed woodland to Devil's Elbow

Gate. The path climbs fairly steeply through the conifer wood for about $^1/_2$ mile. Turn left at the head of the wood and rejoin the main path from Shorts Lane near a wooden seat. Keep left across the moorland slope on a marked path just below and parallel with the main Foxhouse to Sheffield road (A625). About $^1/_2$ mile from a wooden seat, beyond pine woods, you will break out on to the main rhododendron-fringed track. Turn left and follow the wall to an enclosure after about 350 yards. Turn left again through a gate on to the open moor. The path goes forward for 300 yards and then, at the edge of a broken wall and by a sycamore tree, you turn right across the moor. The faint track crosses a stream and keeps to the right by a cascade. Pass another wooden seat and notice. In season bilberries grow in profusion here. Join another main path under Blacka Hill. This path keeps right and descends towards Strawberry Lee Lane via a beech-fringed avenue. There is a car parking area where the track joins the lane. A $^1/_2$ mile stroll along the lane brings you back to Penny Lane and the Cricket Inn. Turn right to the slight incline of the cobbled causeway and return to the start.

POINTS OF INTEREST:
Blacka Moor – These 433 acres were presented to Sheffield City Council in 1933 by the late Alderman J G Graves, the founder of the first mail order credit business. The whole area is maintained by the parks department and is of great natural beauty.

REFRESHMENTS:
The Cross Scythes Inn, (Road Inn) (tel no: 0742 352631).
The Fleur-de-Lys (open all day) (tel no: 0742 361476). Has large car parks and caters for children.
The Cricket Inn, (Penny Lane) (tel no: 0742 365256).
The Crown Inn, (Hillfoot Road) (tel no: 0742 360789).
All the pubs do meals.

Maps: OS Sheets Landranger 110; Pathfinder SK 08/18 & 09/19.

A steep ascent to a moor top path with fine views, then a descent to an easy level track beside the reservoir.

Start: At 173893, the Fairholmes car park.

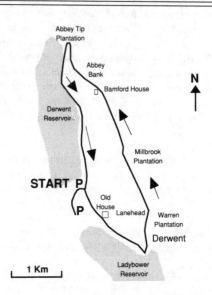

From the car park go to the **Information Centre** and cross the road on to a path. The path cuts off a corner to bring you to the road. Go right below the wall of Derwent reservoir. Keep right around a U-bend and follow the track beside Ladybower Reservoir for nearly a mile. Just before the track makes a sharp left bend, go left up a track to a house called Lanehead. Pass the house and follow the path to the summit of the hill. Where there is a signpost by a wall, the path veers left for a while, then heads straight across the moor.

After crossing another path your way is downhill on Abbey Bank. Nearing the water you enter a narrow wood. Soon you join a track. Go left on this and keep left on the track at the bottom to walk beside Derwent reservoir for about 2 miles to its retaining wall. Go down the bank and right on the road to get back to the car park.

POINTS OF INTEREST:
Information Centre – The Centre, at Fairholmes, has free leaflets containing much about the things of interest in this area including history, nature and sports.

REFRESHMENTS:
Available at Fairholmes car park.

Walk 65   NORBER ERRATICS   6m (9.5km)

Maps: OS Sheets Landranger 98; Outdoor Leisure 2.

An easy climb with fine views and including a visit to the famous Norber Erratics.

Start: At 767684, Austwick.

Leave Austwick by the Horton road and turn left after the school up Town Head Lane. Continue until a crossroad of tracks is reached and turn left for about 50 yards. Take a stone stile on your right and follow the tractor path across the field to reach a gate in a stone wall. Turn right at the wall to follow the footpath for Norber running alongside the wall. At a cross wall go through a stone stile into a sheep gathering pen: leaving immediately by the left-hand wall corner. Keep the wall on your left and follow it as it curves round to your left. On seeing a large stone across the pathway take a path to the right that ascends to a plateau where a signpost to Crummack and Clapham will be seen. Follow the Crummack path which rises to another plateau from where a path on the left takes you up to the Norber Erratics (*see* Walk 32). From the stones a ladder stile in a wall corner to the north takes you on to the open moor. Immediately over the stile turn left and follow the wall for about 100 yards until you see a path rising to your right. Take this path and follow it to the lowest point on the ridge where you will meet a stone wall. At this point there are two routes which can be taken, the first one follows the wall to the right and leads, in about a mile, to a stile on to a path coming up from Clapham. Turn right here to follow the path as it climbs to Long Scar and then down slightly to a junction of three paths. The other alternative gives by far the best views on a clear day: the path follows the cairns along the top of the limestone plateau until a path is reached before the last cairn. Turning right here brings you in a short while to the junction of the three paths. At this junction of paths from Crummack, Selside and Clapham take the right-hand path running in a southerly direction towards Crummack. When the intake wall of Crummack Farm is reached turn right and follow the footpath through two farm gates into Crummack Lane. Follow this lane until a similar lane, signposted to Wharfe, comes in from your left. Take this lane and follow it to Wharfe. On reaching a metalled road turn left to pass through the hamlet of Wharfe. In a few hundred yards a more major road is reached. Turn right on to this road to the first farm track on your left, which is also a bridleway signposted Wood Lane. Follow this track, turning right just before the farm buildings to reach to a walled lane. Keep with the left-hand wall as the right-hand wall deserts the path. The right-hand wall returns to accompany the path on to the main road, ignoring a left-hand loop just before the main road. On the main road turn left to enter Austwick.

REFRESHMENTS:
Whilst Austwick itself has very little to offer in this line, Settle, just 5 miles south-east along the A65, has ample facilities.

Maps: OS Sheets Landranger 110; Pathfinder SE 00/10.

A slightly hilly walk by reservoirs, streams and woods.

Start: The car park at Digley Reservoir.

The car park is signposted from Holme. Go through the gate at the car park end and walk along the southern side of the reservoir. Go across Bilberry Reservoir dam and turn right, uphill, and follow the track and footpaths round the northern side to reach the road by Digley dam. Continue along the road and soon use a small gate on the right. Follow the path left and down to a metalled bridleway. Turn left and walk to Holmbridge. Cross the bridge over the River Holme and turn left along the road signposted to a picnic area. Keep right at a junction and reach a footpath at the end of a group of terraced houses.

Turn left, uphill by the house sides. Before the last, find a small gate on your right giving access to a house drive and a larger gate beyond. Continue uphill with a stream on your right. Cross a wall and turn right, over the stream, and go straight ahead above a gully side. Cross, turn left and pass the end of a short length of wall to reach a stone stile. Turn right along a track and right again along a smaller track downhill. Use the field side if it is easier at first, but rejoin the track as soon as it improves. The track turns right and then left, crosses an open field and reaches a group of houses. Pass between these to reach the road above Brownhill Reservoir.

Turn left and follow the road through the trees above Ramsden Reservoir. The road crosses the dam of Riding Wood Reservoir and soon bends left. If you wish to see Yateholme Reservoir, continue ahead for a short distance and then return. Cross the stone stile on the right, at the bend, walk straight downhill between trees and go through a gap in the wall ahead. Turn left and cross the footbridge below. Go uphill above the stream and Ramsden Reservoir. Cross a ladder stile on your right, and turn left along the footpath. This turns left and down into a valley, goes over a footbridge by a waterfall, up the opposite side and enters a field. Bear left, uphill, to cross two stone stiles and soon a wooden stile on your left. Pass through a gate and reach the road at **Holme**.

Turn left past the access road, and turn right over cobbles. Go along the lane bearing right. Pass through a gate downhill from the open gateway ahead. Follow the trodden path over and through stiles eventually bearing right. Turn right to reach Digley Reservoir and retrace your steps to the car park.

POINTS OF INTEREST:
Holme – Gives its name to the valley in 'Last of the Summer Wine' country. The walk passes through the main water gathering area and at one point gives good views of nearby Holmfirth. Holme Moss transmitter is often seen.

REFRESHMENTS:
Places are plentiful with pubs in Holme, Holmbridge and Holmfirth. A café can also be found in the latter.

Walk 67   **DUKE OF DEVONSHIRE'S LEAD MINES**   6m (10km)
Maps: OS Sheets Landranger 98; Pathfinder SE 06/16.
Moderate, but care is needed.
Start: At 025632, on the roadside near Hebden.

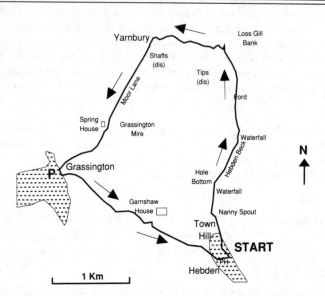

Walking along the track through the old lead mines is straightforward. However, there are many ruins and abandoned workings, so it would be prudent to keep children and dogs under control for this part of the walk. Cross the B6265 and go up the lane beside Hebden Beck. The tall building on the left was once a cotton mill. In Spring there are primroses down the banks, and the cuckoo can be heard: in Summer there is the heady scent of meadowsweet. As you go up the lane, Nanny Spout waterfall can be glimpsed off to the right. Go past cottages and over a packhorse bridge. The lane now becomes a track: continue to the site of the loading yard where you can see the remains of setts, or paving. Ford the stream at its shallowest point and continue upstream. Dippers can be seen hereabouts. The hillocks to the left are spoil heaps, thinly covered with grass, and the track winds round them to the hilltop. On the skyline can be seen the smelting chimney. Follow the track past bell pits to a clump of trees and cottages. This is

Yarnbury and there are now holiday cottages, where once there were the mine manager's home and office, and a row of houses for other officials. The building to the right was the blacksmith's shop, and in the grounds are the remains of the gunpowder store. Turn left and go down the steep land to **Grassington**.

After exploring the delightful village of Grassington return up Main Street to the Town Hall and Devonshire Institute. Turn right, then take the first turning left into High Lane. Pause to look back at Grassington's roofscape. You are now in a Green Lane which can be muddy. Herb Robert grows in the cracks of the drystone walls. Continue along the lane, which later becomes a path, with stiles. When the old Grassington Hospital is reached, the path continues across the lawn in front of it to a gap in the wall. Beyond it descends gently over fields and stiles to a lane, and on to the B6265. Cross the road and go down to the crossroads and your starting point.

POINTS OF INTEREST:
Grassington – Once the centre of the lead mining industry. It has many interesting folds, or yards. There is a National Parks Centre, and a variety of shops, inns and eating places. The Congregational Church was built in 1812.

REFRESHMENTS:
Numerous in Grassington.

Walk 68   SHIPLEY GLEN AND 5 RISE LOCKS   6m (10km)

Maps: OS Sheets Landranger 104; Pathfinder SE 04/14 & 03/13.
A beautiful wooded valley and fascinating stretch of canal.
Start: The open space on the east bank of the Leeds–Liverpool
Canal on Primrose Lane, off the A650.

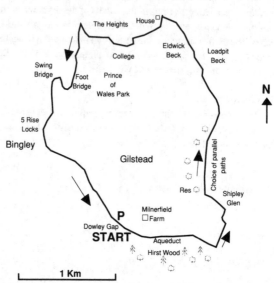

Cross the canal bridge near the Fisherman's Inn. Turn left along the towpath and walk
past locks. Cross a bridge to the opposite bank where the towpath also changes over.
The canal crosses the River Aire by means of an aqueduct. Reach a second group of
locks and turn left at their centre. Go down a few steps and over a footbridge across the
river. Continue ahead, slightly uphill, between houses. Cross a road and bear slightly
left along an enclosed footpath. At the junction soon reached, turn left through the edge
of the woodland. An easy wide path bears right, up **Shipley Glen**. Alternatively, bear
left at a junction down to a footbridge and small reservoir. Do not cross, but turn right
and follow a choice of narrow, slightly more difficult paths uphill by the side of Loadpit
Beck and up the Glen, keeping below the larger rocks. Eventually, either way, a more
open area is reached near a footpath sign pointing down to a stone sided bridge over

the beck. Cross over the bridge, and walk ahead along the wide track and Saltaire Road, with the beck on your right.

Turn right at the main road and walk the short distance down to The Green on your left. Continue down here past the Acorn Inn. The lane becomes a track with a sometimes rough surface. Turn left at a junction and pass another junction on the right. The track turns left past Tewitt House and reaches a road by Lower Heights Farm. Turn left for a few yards, then cross the road and pass through a gate on the right to walk through a small field and between buildings. Bear right across the larger field reached towards the far right-hand corner. Cross the stone stile and walk by the wall side for two fields, above buildings of the former Bingley College. Cross a stone stile reached on the left, and bear right to a road. Keep straight ahead, to the right of a mini roundabout, to reach a main road.

Turn right along the road, passing Greenhill Crag Farm. Immediately on reaching the road junction at Greenhill, turn left through a kissing gate and follow the path downhill along the fence side. Maintain direction through more kissing gates and across a track, and go between houses to reach a road. Cross and walk down Pinedale to where the track continues, crossing a lane and going down a few steps. Reach and turn right along Beck Lane. Turn left at the roundabout and cross over the **Leeds–Liverpool Canal**. Turn left and walk back along the towpath passing the **5 Rise Locks** and going through the centre of Bingley to reach the start.

POINTS OF INTEREST:

Shipley Glen – A noted local beauty spot with its stream and beautiful woodland. Disused quarries at the top and large rocks help to make it an adventure area for children.

Leeds–Liverpool Canal – Still much used, particularly by pleasure craft. A 'water bus' may be found operating along one section of the canal on the walk.

5 Rise Locks – Unique. The canal rises a considerable height along the valley side. Moorings here ensure that there are plenty of boats to see.

REFRESHMENTS:

The Fisherman's Inn (tel no: 0274 564238).
The Acorn Inn, (tel no: 0274 561549).
As well as being plentiful in Bingley.

Walk 69   HARDEN AND ST IVES   6m (10km)

Maps: OS Sheets Landranger 104; Pathfinder SE 03/13.

Fairly easy walking from a small industrial town through beautiful estate land, woodland, and to an excellent viewpoint.
Start: The Wilsden Road, Harden.

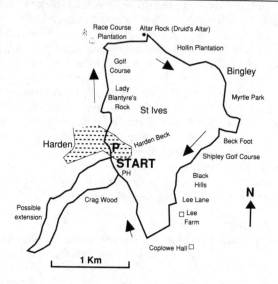

Walk north and cross to Keighley road. Follow this uphill to a left bend and turn right into the **St Ives Estate**. A short distance along the drive, turn left up steps and go along a path. Reach a T-junction. If you wish, divert right to see the lake and return to the junction, otherwise turn left and follow the path as it bears right, close to Lady Blantyre's Rock and then left by the side of woodland. Bear right at a junction, keeping to the edge of the trees and, shortly, past the corner of a golf course. Take a path to the right, a little distance from the boundary wall, which passes through Race Course Plantation. The path emerges out of the plantation, passes through a gate, and goes straight on to a gate in the boundary wall. Pass through, turn left, through a second gate, and bear slightly left, across Altar Lane and a little rough and open land to reach the **Altar Rock**. From it there are excellent views of industrial Airedale below.

Turn right and take a path bearing away from the hill edge to regain Altar Lane by Hollin Plantation. Follow the lane down to reach the edge of Bingley. Cross Harden Road and take the narrow track through woodland downhill to reach a field. Cross the footbridge over the River Aire ahead and turn right along the bank, through Myrtle Park. Just past the junction with Harden Beck, cross a second footbridge and walk along the enclosed path to a lane. Turn right to Beck Foot. Cross the footbridge over the beck and go over two stiles to regain the lane. Just before a house, turn left, down steps and over a bridge. Cross Shipley Golf Course, being wary of golfers, and bear right to pass to the right of a small group of trees aiming for the boundary fence just to the right of the far corner, near the edge of woodland. Find and cross a stile and bear left soon along a clearer path to reach a small gate. Pass through and follow the rough track uphill through the wood ignoring other gates, to reach a stone stile. Across the field beyond is a squeeze stile. Bear left from it to the corner of the next field and go over a stile. An enclosed path turns right: follow the wallside to Lee Lane. Just to the left, pass through the left-hand of two gateways opposite and bear half-left to a stile. Maintain direction to a second stile emerge on to Cross Lane. Turn right and go down a track to houses. Turn right through a gate and go along a footpath. Reach Sandy Banks, a wide track, and turn left, down to Wilsden Road. Turn right and follow the road back into Harden.

POINTS OF INTEREST:

St Ives Estate – A very pleasant parkland, much of which is used as a golf course. Woods add to the attraction.

Altar Rock – Reputed to have been used by the Druids for sacrifices, but no proof has been established.

REFRESHMENTS:

The Malt Shovel Inn, Wilsden Road (tel no: 0535 272357). Close to the beck bridge. Can also be obtained by diverting into Bingley.

MICKLEDEN   7m (12km)

Maps: OS Sheets Landranger 110; Pathfinder SK 09/19, 29/39,
SE 00/10 & 20/30.

A fine moorland walk .

Start: The Wagon and Horses Inn, Langsett.

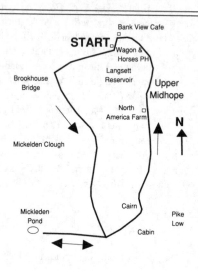

Head for the signposted forest path to the right of Langsett Reservoir. After a mile the
Don river appears at Brookhouse Bridge. Ascend the cut gate track (a bridleway to
Upper Derwent and well signed), cross Brookhouse Bridge and go over Hingcliff
Common. About $1^1/_2$ miles from the bridge you reach the heights of Mickleden Edge.
At the side of the path the waters of Mickleden Spring accompany you. Just below and
to the right of the spring is a walled enclosure called Deadman's Wall which was
reputed to be a local burial ground. Also across the stream and hidden under a fold of
Bradshaw Hill are the ruins of Tom's Bower or 'Tom's Boure', where Tom Crossley
often rested during the 17th century while shepherding his flock on the hills. A few
hundred yards to the south is Mickleden Pond which, according to tradition, covers an
abandoned silver mine. Return to Mickleden Edge and the signpost where the tracks

from Brookhouse and Upper Midhope meet. Walk 600 yards due east from the signpost and you will see the ruins of another ancient shelter hidden in the bracken. Jossie Sanderson constructed this cabin around 1700. His grave can be found in Midhopestone's churchyard. Turn north for 300 yards and stroll back to the track leading to Upper Midhope. Head for Thickwood Lane and the hamlet of Upper Midhope. Keep to the left by the side of Townend Farm, the old homestead of the Sanderson family. A short stroll down the lane and keeping to the left brings you back to the shores of Langsett Reservoir. The road skirts Midhope Cliff and the embankment of Sheffield's water supply and you are soon back at Langsett village.

REFRESHMENTS:

The Wagon and Horses, Langsett (tel: 0226 763147). Caters for children.

The Bank View Café, Langsett (tel no: 0226 762337). Has a shop and offers full meals.

Walk 71   ILKLEY MOOR   7m (12km)

Maps: OS Sheets Landranger 104; Pathfinder SE 04/14.

A walk over open moorland with a touch of history.

Start: The moorside road south of the college in Ilkley.

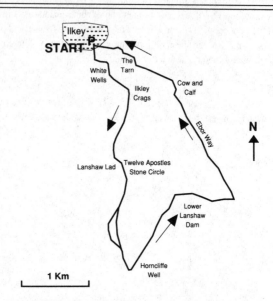

From the nearby **White Wells Museum** car park, a path crossing a stream with waterfalls leads up to the museum. Behind and a little to the right of the museum, a track bears left, uphill, towards Ilkley Crags. Occasionally steps help with climb: ignore all small paths off and tracks crossed. Cairns mark our route to a boundary stone, Lanshaw Lad. Soon after the Twelve Apostles Stone Circle is reached on our left. A boundary wall is soon seen ahead and, a little before it, a not too clear footpath leads off to the left to reach the wall at a stile. Alternatively, continue to the wall, cross a stile, and turn left by the wall to the correct stile.

A track now leads a little away from the wall, downhill. Reach a fence on the opposite side of the wall and two stiles. Cross the stile on the right to look at Horncliffe Well and the stones around, then re-cross and use the stile on the left. A narrow footpath soon takes you a few yards away from the fence but generally runs parallel to it. Cross small streams with care. Continue along the clear path through the heather after passing the corner of the fence to reach an old railway carriage. Cross a track and, slightly to the right, take the narrow path which leads down to pass to the left of Lower Lanshaw Dam, a small reservoir. Keep to the left of a boundary marker as you walk downhill. The path bears left and reaches a wider track. Turn left and soon fork right to cross the stream in the valley. Turn right, going steadily uphill along the main track after crossing, and walk downhill to a junction. Turn left to follow a wallside track. You are now on the Ebor Way.

Hangingstone Road is soon below, but keep to the track just above the steeper part of the hillside. The Cow and Calf Hotel and rocks are seen ahead. Bear right along a narrower path downhill just before the hotel. Generally maintain direction towards the rocks which disappear from view for a short distance: don't worry, most paths lead you to them. Descend to pass between the isolated Calf and the larger Cow. Continue slightly down to reach a wider track going uphill. Before reaching a fence, turn right along a path heading for the now visible Tarn. Soon the path crosses a valley with a footbridge over a stream. Reach the Tarn and continue along the surfaced track by its side and downhill towards houses. Turn left just before these up to a wooden shelter and then bear left downhill, across a footbridge, to the road and your car.

POINTS OF INTEREST:
White Wells Museum – Open during the summer on Saturdays and Sundays 11–5.

REFRESHMENTS:
Available from inns and cafés in Ilkley.

Maps: OS Sheets Landranger 103; Outdoor Leisure 21.
Industrial heritage, steep sided valleys with steady climbs, canal side and old tracks.
Start: The Rochdale Canal, Union Street South, Todmorden.

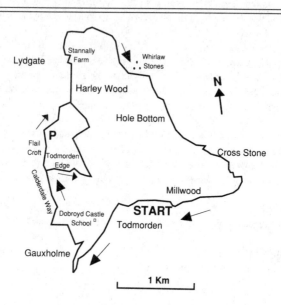

Turn right, along the canal towpath to the Rochdale Road bridge. Pass below and cross to continue on the opposite bank. Pass a series of locks and go under the interesting railway bridge before going under a road bridge at Gauxholme. Cross by the lock, and turn right to cross the road. Walk straight ahead, uphill, along Pexwood Road. There are excellent views before you reach a junction with the entry to Dobroyd Castle School. Turn left, along Stones Road and the **Calderdale Way**, soon turning sharp right to pass Lob Quarry. The road becomes a rougher track and passes between a wall and a fence. Pass through a gate and turn left off the track and uphill by the side of a wall. Go over several stiles to reach Parkin Lane. Turn left and, at the bend, turn right along a track. The Way goes off to the right, but you continue ahead past the stables, going to the left of the two main buildings of Flail Croft. Turn right between the buildings and go through the gate to the right of a horse training area. Pass round this and follow the wall side downhill to reach the tree covered Todmorden Edge. Cross the low fence in the field corner and bear left, steadily descending the steep hillside on a slightly difficult grass path through the trees. (Anyone not liking this type of descent can avoid it by turning left, earlier, at Parkin Lane and turning left along the narrower road reached and soon rejoin the Way.)

At the bottom of the hill, turn right along the narrow lane, and go straight across the Burnley Road. Rejoin the Way, walking up Stoney Royd Lane which passes under a railway bridge and to the left of Stannally Farm, before reaching a small stream with waterfalls. Keep to the left of a house and reach a track junction near the top of the hill. Turn right. The track becomes a paved 'trod' which bears left below Whirlaw Stones and again becomes a track. Soon, turn right, downhill, along the now tarmacked lane. Keep left at a junction, and continue ahead where the Way turns left at a stile. The track passes by the side of a golf course before reaching a road. Turn right, downhill, and left at a T-junction. Just before the ruined church at Cross Stone, turn sharp right at the side of a viewing area, down a narrow path, quickly turning sharp left down steps. Follow the enclosed path downhill going straight ahead at a path junction. Reach houses and a rough road. Bear left along the improving road, and right along a 'No Entry' entry section to reach the A646. Turn left and cross. Turn right at Woodhouse Lane, signposted 'Mankinholes'. Cross the River Calder and take the steps on the left down to the canal. Turn right and follow the canal back to **Todmorden** and the start.

POINTS OF INTEREST:

Calderdale Way – The 50 miles long Way circles the dale between Halifax and Todmorden. Waymarked with a 'tree' symbol.

Todmorden – Developed during the industrial revolution, well placed at a valley junction. As with many local valleys, river, canal, and railway fill much of the space. The Rochdale Canal has been very well restored, and attracts wildfowl.

REFRESHMENTS:

Plentiful from the many inns and shops along the valley roads.

Walk 73   SIX OLD HALLS AROUND TOTLEY   8m (13km

Maps: OS Sheets Landranger 119; Outdoor Leisure 24.

An easy and delightful walk through woods and fields to locate
some fine old halls on the outskirts of Sheffield.

Start: The Post Office, Totley Hall Lane, Totley.

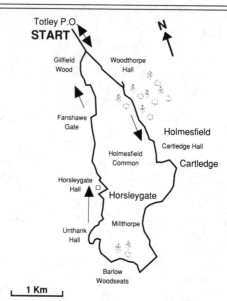

Walk along Totley Hall Lane for 400 yards to the Polytechnic College entrance. Go
over a stile on the left and across two fields. Keep ahead to Gillfield Wood and reach
a white wooden bridge over the infant Totley Brook, a principal feeder of the River
Sheaf. Cross and follow a path that rises across Shepherds Hill to reach the side of the
first mansion house, **Woodthorpe Hall**, viewed from the lane just beyond an iron gate.
Turn right along the lane for 300 yards to join another path going into Holmesfield Park
Wood. After 1 mile join the lane into Holmesfield village which seems to boast more
pubs than houses. Cross the road by the Angel Inn. A fingerpost points into the
Cordwell Valley by the side of the George and Dragon Inn. Cross two fields to a stile
and a footbridge, left, towards the hamlet of Cartledge. A steep pull up a field reaches
the road between Holmesfield and Millthorpe. Turn left for 75 yards to reach

148

Cartledge Hall. Cross the lane and take the path through Cartledge Farm. Negotiate two field stiles as you descend to the Cordwell Valley. Join the road, left into Millthorpe. The Royal Oak Inn at the cross roads is ideal for bar lunches. At the crossroads go ahead into a lane by the Barlow Brook (ford) and join a field path to the left which leads to Johnnygate Farm. Rejoin a lane right for 400 yards and view the third hall, **Barlow Woodseats**.

After leaving the hall take the field path directly across to Rose Wood and Meekfields. Locate a rickety wooden stile after the third field, by keeping to the centre of the last field – there are no markers. Cross the stile and enter Rose Wood. Keep ahead for 600 yards to Meekfields. Cross two fields to Unthank Lane. Turn left for 350 yards to **Unthank Hall**. Cross the lane to another field – be sure to shut the gate – and after the first field bear right and descend across two fields to the Barlow Brook and Eweford Bridge. Across the bridge join a bridleway: a fingerpost points the way to Horsleygate Lane. Turn right from the road and in 250 yards you will see **Horsleygate Hall** on the left. Just above the hall, and opposite a private caravan site, another fingerpost points the way to Lidgate and Totley. Cross two fields and a large open stretch of ploughed field following yellow markers. Cross the road at Lidgate (below the Robin Hood Inn) and another signpost points to Totley and the last hall, **Fanshawe Gate**. By the side of a huge ash tree reputed to be nearly 600 years old another fingerpost points the way for the last mile back to Totley across meadows, through Gillfield wood and across pastures bordering Strawberry Fields.

POINTS OF INTEREST:

Woodthorpe Hall – Home of the Shepley family.

Cartledge Hall – Dates from the 15th century. Reputed to be haunted from the days of Elizabeth I.

Barlow Woodseats – Used to offer afternoon tea in the 1930s for one shilling!

Unthank Hall – Now run as a farm. John Lowe may let you see the fine cruck barn at the rear of the hall.

Horsleygate Hall – Home of the Ponsford family and recently converted to a high standard from its 15th century days.

Fanshaw Gate – Home of the Ramsden family and the oldest mansion in the district. The dovecote extension dates back to the 12th century.

REFRESHMENTS:
Numerous!, and most of which do meals.

Maps: OS Sheets Landranger 98; Outdoor Leisure 10.
A steep pull out of Settle and a steep descent at the finish.
Start: At 819637, a car park in Settle.

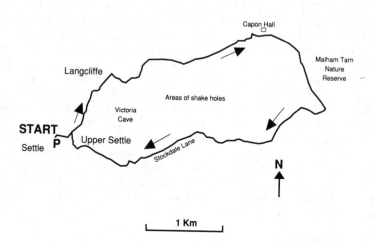

To reach the start take the road through the centre of Settle. Where the road turns sharp left into the High Street, look for the parking sign on the left. Set off from the far end of the car park, past the toilets, and turn right along a passage-way to the Market. Cross the main road. Facing you is a row of colonnaded shops with cottages above. Go to the left of these and up steep Constitution Hill. The road turns left at the end of the houses. Look for a stony, walled lane going up to the right. At the top, pause for breath and the view. **Settle** is below you, the green dome of Giggleswick School chapel is across the valley. If you look down to the right you will see Langcliffe, the Settle-Carlisle railway and the River Ribble.

    Keep to the track across fields, ignoring a path up to the right. A narrow road can be seen coming up from Langcliffe: our path ascends to the lower edge of a wood and continues to join this road at a bend. Turn right and follow a gated lane up the edge of the wood. Limestone scars are in front of you and there is another fine view back across the valley. Go past a fingerpost to Victoria Cave. Follow the lane over the hill to where it ends abruptly and go forward on a path with the wall on your left. Go through a gateway beyond which the path is indistinct. Keep in the same direction, with Black Hill on your right and descend by a wall to the road at Capon Hall. Turn right. Where the road forks at a cattle grid, turn right and right again at the next fork. **Malham Tarn** can be seen to the left, while in the foreground is a ruined smelting chimney. Watch out for traffic on these narrow roads: Malham is a popular area.

Go down to Langscar Gate, cross the cattle grid, and turn right on the rough track. Go up to a gateway. Go through and take the path uphill to Nappa Cross, set in a drystone wall. A path comes up from the left through a gate, join this and go to the right. Though this is a definite track, it is very stony. Follow it down the side of a steep valley, with Rye Loaf Hill to the left. Beyond Stockdale Farm the walking is easier. This is high limestone country, with scars and canyons – Altermire Scar to the right – and after heavy rain, the underground water jets and bubbles into streams and pools. The lane takes you down to a road. Turn right and, taking care as before, follow it to Settle. From the top of the final descent, there is a bird's-eye view of the town.

POINTS OF INTEREST:

Settle – A market town, with various inns and cafés. The Folly, a 17th century house, is so called because it was too expensive for its builder to complete.

Malham Tarn – Usually, water drains through the limestone. There is a tarn here because there is a saucer of impervious Silurian slate. At Tarn House, Charles Kingsley wrote part of 'The Water Babies'.

REFRESHMENTS:

The 'Old Naked Man' Café, Settle (tel no: 07292 32030). A warm welcome for walkers.

Walk 75   THROUGH THE CORDWELL VALLEY   8m (13km)

Maps: OS Sheets Landranger 119; Pathfinder SK 28/38 & 27/37.
Delightful field, woodland and moorland paths.
Start: Totley Hall Lane, Totley.

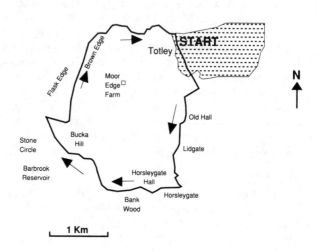

1 Km

Walk along Totley Hall Lane past the college grounds to the start of two field paths to Gillfield Wood. Cross the infant Totley Brook via a white wooden bridge. About 100 yards from the bridge negotiate a stile on the right and follow a path skirting the woodland glade. After 250 yards cross another stile into a field. About 300 yards further the path steepens to the left towards the charming old mansion house of Fanshaw Gate (*see* Walk 73). Note the massive ash tree as you enter the lane. Go right past the hall and join another field path (fingerpost) on the left, to the hamlet of Lidgate. Cross the B6054 to a fingerpost pointing the way down in to the Cordwell Valley. Yellow markers guide you along field paths to Horsleygate Hall and lane via field paths. Turn right down the lane for 450 yards to a field path on the left with a signpost. Cross the B6051 (Chesterfield to Owler Bar road) to a signpost and stone stile. Climb over the stile and go into Smeekley Woods. Follow the Barlow Brook and the main path to the right as far as Car Lane and the water treatment plant.

Head right up a steep rough track for 500 yards to reach open moorland – Ramsley Moor recently purchased by the National Park Authority – on the right. The path climbs fairly steeply over lovely heather and bilberry slopes for $^2/_3$ mile to reach the main Sheffield to Baslow road, the A621. Cross with care to reach Big Moor through a large white gate. Markers on posts point out the route which bears right for nearly a mile across the moor. Note the Barbrook Reservoir, the breeding ground of many rare birds. Join the B6054 via a stone stile and walk right for 100 yards. Cross the road and enter Totley Moss by a kissing gate. Don't forget to replace the chain over the stone post. Walk parallel with the road edge by the side of the wall for 200 yards, then swing over to the left along a well-defined track under Flask Edge. Note the huge stone cairn that dominates the skyline. After 1 mile the path descends under Brown Edge. Rejoin the main path to Totley via field paths above the Totley rifle range or by Rough Lane into Moss Road via Bolehill Lodge*. Descend Moss Road, past the rifle range club house, turn left along Lane Head Road and enter the sports field on the right. Walk to the Cricket Inn, then follow Penny Lane and the cobbled causeway on the right back to Hillfoot Road and the finish of the walk.

*An alternative route from Bolehill Lodge is to walk straight from the top of Moss Road on to a rough track and down to Strawberry Lee Lane end. Turn right and walk back to the sports field via Penny Lane.

REFRESHMENTS:
The Cross Scythes Inn, (Road Inn) (tel no: 0742 352631).
The Fleur-de-Lys (open all day) (tel no: 0742 361476). Has large car parks and caters for children.
The Cricket Inn, (Penny Lane) (tel no: 0742 365256).
The Crown Inn, (Hillfoot Road) (tel no: 0742 360789).
The Robin Hood Inn, Lidgate (tel no: 0742 890360). First class meals.

Walk 76   CARL WARK AND NETHER PADLEY   8m (13km)

Maps: OS Sheets Landranger 110 & 119; Outdoor Leisure 24.
*Moderate climbing and a little easy scrambling. Moorland,
woodland and a gorge add to the variety on this fascinating walk.*
Start: On the A625 Sheffield–Hathersage road, just to the west of
Toad's Mouth.

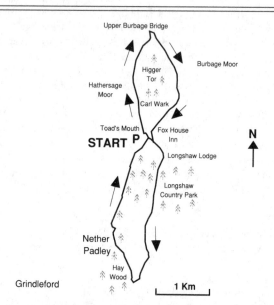

From this unusually shaped rock, take the footpath north on the western bank of the
stream and climb up to **Carl Wark**. Continue slightly west of north to reach and follow
the eroded track up to **Higger Tor**. The promised easy scramble is needed to gain the
top. Look just to the north to find and follow a path, west of the stream, that leads to
the road at the head of the valley. Cross the bridge and turn right along the wide track
back to the A625. Turn left uphill to the B6521. You may wish to find refreshment
ahead at Fox Inn before turning along the road. The entry to **Longshaw Lodge** is soon
reached on your left. Walk along the track keeping west of the Lodge and avoid straying
on to minor paths. Reach the B6054 and turn right for a little road walking.

  A gate is reached on the right just after the road starts to descend the hill off the

154

edge. Go through and walk along the path, which passes through The Haywood. Do not descend at the first path junction. The higher path descends steadily to reach a road in Nether Padley. Continue downhill in the same direction along the road. Reach and cross the B6521 where a path goes down to **Grindleford Station**. Turn right at the bottom of this path to reach a bridge over Burbage Brook. Do not cross. On your right, find the almost hidden entry to **Padley Gorge**. There are plenty of paths to explore here, but it is easiest to take the path upwards, climbing steadily to reach a gate by a road. Continue on the path ahead which is a little rough on occasions and has a mini hill but eventually reaches the eastern bank of the brook and open ground. The brook can be followed on either side although the western bank is best for the return to your car at the road ahead.

POINTS OF INTEREST:

Carl Wark – This rocky area has the remains of an Iron Age fort. It is an excellent viewpoint.

Higger Tor – A natural rock formation that also gives excellent views.

Longshaw Lodge – Within Longshaw Country Park. There is an Information Centre here.

Grindleford Station – Has a useful café frequented by walkers and cyclists. There are good mugs of tea. Trains frequently can be seen disappearing into Totley tunnel here. Some also emerge! The line goes to Hope and Edale and is of great value to walkers.

Padley Gorge – A popular play area for children. There is a nature trail.

REFRESHMENTS:

The Fox House Inn, (tel no: 0433 30374).

Café at Grindleford Station – see above.

Maps: OS Sheets Landranger 104; Outdoor Leisure 10.
If access to Barden Fell is restricted, as it is during droughts there will be notices posted.
Start: The car park at 071539.

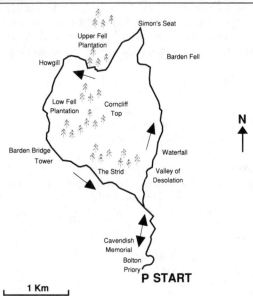

Please note: dogs are not allowed on the fell as it is a game-bird breeding area. Leave the car park and turn left on the main road into the village. Note the tithe barn opposite. Go past the Post Office tearooms and through the hole in the wall to the grounds of **Bolton Priory**. Go down to the River Wharfe, passing the ruins, and up to the Cavendish Memorial. Follow the lane down and right to the next car park by the Cavendish Pavilion snack bar. Cross the river by the footbridge and turn left on the narrow Storiths road. At the top of the first rise in the road there is a wicket gate in the stone wall on your right. Go through, pass the cottage and follow the path up to Posforth Gill. The path ascends steeply by a waterfall to a delightful spot called the Valley of Desolation.

Cross the stream by the footbridge and follow the path to a fork. If you wish to see the next waterfall, take the right fork. You will have to return as there is no access to the fell. The left-hand path goes up to a gate and stile. Go over and follow the forestry road up and right, through the plantation to a gate which brings you out on to the moor. Follow the track across a ford and up past a stone table to cross the head of the beck. From here follow the cairns to the largest jumble of millstone grit boulders. This group is called Simon's Seat, perched on the edge of an escarpment and with a good view up Wharfedale.

Turn left, on a broad track which descends gradually through the heather to a plantation. Turn right down a steep lane to Howgill. Go straight across the narrow road and follow a walled path down to the Storiths road. Cross, then follow the riverside path down to Barden Bridge. Pass the bridge and continue along the river with **Barden Tower** on the opposite bank.

Soon, the path ascends to woodland. Down to the right, the Strid can be seen – the river is forced into this narrow channel, causing undercurrents and whirlpools. The path goes up to the road and soon you come to the wooden footbridge by the Cavendish Pavilion. Go over and return to the start.

POINTS OF INTEREST:
Bolton Priory – Founded in 1120 and beautifully situated. The nave of the priory church is used as a parish church.
Barden Tower – A tall, fortified manor house built about 1485.

REFRESHMENTS:
There is a café and shop serving the caravan site at Howgill. It is a few yards to the right of the Howgill crossroads.

Walk 78   HIGH ROAD TO FOX HOUSE $9\frac{1}{2}$ m (15km)

Maps: OS Sheets Landranger 110 & 119; Pathfinder SK 28/38 & Outdoor Leisure 24.

A fine moorland walk on easy paths with glorious views.

Start: Totley bus terminus.

From the bus terminus proceed right down Hillfoot Road. About 150 yards along the road, at a bend, turn left into Chapel Lane. Follow the cobbled causeway across a field to Penny Lane. Turn left and enter a sports field at the side of the Cricket Inn. Cross the field to Strawberry Lee Lane and after $\frac{1}{2}$ mile join a bridle track through a lovely beech tree avenue that fringes Blacka Moor. The track ascends Blacka Hill for a further $\frac{3}{4}$ mile and passes several wooden seats. The track leads to a gate and the ruined farmstead of Strawberry Lee. Locate two stone pillars and a broken footpath sign and walk over the crest of the hill to the left. A slight cairned track goes to a wall and a stile on to Totley Moss. Turn right and take the well-defined track for $\frac{1}{2}$ mile to Stony Ridge Road. Cross the road and go over a ladder stile on to Stony Ridge Moor. Take the path – it is level for $\frac{1}{4}$ mile and then descends to the A625 via another ladder stile. Turn left for 300 yards to take a break at the Fox House Inn.

Cross the road just below the inn and go through a gate into the Longshaw estate, owned by the National Trust. Head past the lodge and hall and pass a line of rhododendron bushes where you swing over to the left to join another broad track which passes Little John's Well. This track joins the Froggatt–Calver road. Cross on to White Edge Moor where a fingerpost directs you to **White Edge Lodge**. Locate a stile at the crest of the hill, to the left just above the lodge, and go over on to Big Moor. Keep forward to the ancient **Lady's Cross**. Markers point the route past tumuli and old guide stones to Barbrook Bridge and the Owler Bar, B6054, road, reached by a ladder stile. Walk right, along the road for 150 yards and go through a gate on the left on to Totley Moss. Follow a faint track across the moor for 1 mile with Flask Edge on the right. (Note the rail tunnel air shaft over to the left.) Turn right along the broad track between Brown Edge and Bolehill and walk on to a bridleway via a gate. Descend steep fields 50yds from the gate via a wooden stile on the right at the side of Totley Rifle Range. (Red flags are positioned when firing is in progress but there is no danger: these paths are Rights of Way and open at all times.) After crossing two more stiles join Moss Road. Walk down the road to Lane Head Road and turn left for 75 yards to reach Totley sports field above the Cricket Inn. Turn right off Penny Lane and retrace your steps via the cobbled causeway and Hillfoot Road to the start of the walk.

POINTS OF INTEREST:
White Edge Lodge – An ex-gamekeeper's lodge now an outward bound centre.
Lady's Cross – Associated with monks of Beauchief Abbey near Sheffield.

REFRESHMENTS:
The Fox House Inn, (tel no: 0433 30374).
And the inns around Totley.

Walk 79   SHEFFIELD'S GREEN BELT   10m (16km)

Maps: OS Sheets Landranger 110; Pathfinder SK 28/38.

A scenic walk in woodland and on moorland.

Start: Mill Lane, Totley.

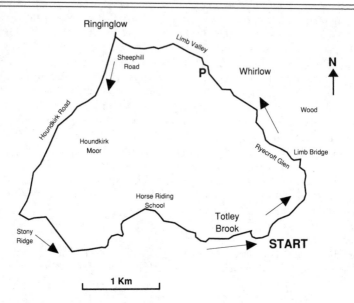

From Mill Lane take a signed path into Poynton Wood via a footbridge over Totley Brook. After $^1/_2$ mile the path dips towards an iron fence above a railway line. Go over a stile to a broad track to Twenty Well Lane. Cross the road via the rail bridge and take a gennel which runs behind a block of garages to Dore Rail Station. Cross the station yard into Abbeydale Road South. Pass a garden centre and on the opposite side of the road enter **Ecclesall Woods**. Follow a signed bridle path along Limb Brook. After $^1/_2$ mile go right towards Limb Valley and Whirlow. About $^1/_2$ mile on is a stile. Go over and cross sports fields to Limb Lane. Cross the busy A625 with care to reach Whirlow Brook Park. Follow the drive to the hall and gate into woodland: follow a path behind the hall and by a car park. Join a main path into the Limb Valley. Go through the woods for $1^1/_2$ miles towards the hamlet of Ringinglow. Cross a field on a stone causeway and another field to a stile on to Sheephill Road. Go along Sheephill Road for 100 yards to where the road bends to join the start of the Hound Kirk Track. Follow this old turnpike road for over 2 miles between the moors of Hound Kirk and Burbage. After a second and final gate the track descends towards Fox House and the outdoor pursuits centre of the Parsons House. Go left towards the ruined farm of Stony Ridge. Walk left again for 250 yards along the A625 passing a toll bar boundary stone. Cross the road with care into Blacka Moor. A broad track fringes a line of rhododendron bushes, then crosses an open moor for $1/_2$ mile. Go through a gate and descend towards the ruined farm of Strawberry Lee. Another gate gives access to Totley Moor where, at a fork, signs point down into Blacka Moor. Follow these to join the main path descending from Piper House Gate to the Fashionable Dore Horse Riding School along Shorts Lane. At a corner a fingerpost points out a field route to Avenue Farm. Go over two stiles by the side of the old Hay Brook and join another lane. About 250 yards beyond Avenue Farm turn right into Hillfoot Road. Walk another 300 yards and turn left to a field path by the side of a high walled residence. A final stile crosses the Old Hay Brook once again to Totley Brook road. Keep forward for another 450 yards and cross a railway footbridge into Grove road. Turn left to the start.

POINTS OF INTEREST:
Ecclesall Woods – Incorporating bird sanctuary, model railway circuit, picnic areas.

REFRESHMENTS:
The Shepley Spitfire Hotel, Mickley Lane, Totley (tel no: 0742 360298). Bars meals.
The Old Mother Redcap Inn, Prospect Road, Bradway (tel no: 0742 360179). Bar meals.
The Norfolk Arms Inn, Ringinglow Road (tel no: 0742 302197). Bar meals etc.
The Whirlow Brook Park Hall, (tel no: 0742 759852). Full catering facilities and café. Large parties, weddings etc. Conference centre.
The Beauchief Hotel, Abbeydale Road South (tel no: 0742 620500). A three star hotel, high class accommodation facilities.
The Castle Inn, 20 Well Lane, Bradway (tel no: 0742 362955). Bar meals.
The Rising Sun Hotel, Abbey Lane (tel no: 0742 360778). Full meals. High class.

Maps: OS Sheets Landranger 103 & 104; Outdoor Leisure 10.
*A very spectacular walk, offering superb views. Quite strenuous
and can be muddy on the tops.*
Start: Embsay car park.

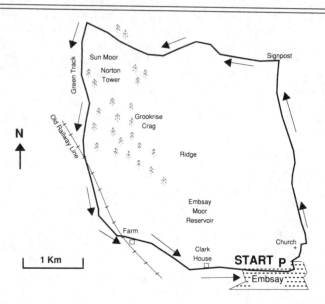

Leave the rear of the car park, going over a stile and diagonally right to reach a road
to the south of the church via some stone stiles and a gate. Turn left, along the road, past
the church and 70 yards after the road turns sharp right, go left along a path signed
'Embsay Crag and Reservoir'. Continue along a farm road to Boncraft Farm, and there
keep straight ahead along a track to a gate. Go through and along a path, keeping close
to a wall on the left. Pass a wood and reach moorland through a gate. Now bear right,
following yellow waymarkers northwards, along a moorland path with distant Deer
Sallows Ridge to the left. After about 1¹/₂ miles a more distinct track crosses your line
of walk at a signpost. Turn left along it, going towards Rylstone with good views of
Simons' Seat in Wharfedale and Lancashire's Pendle Hill.

Continue along this broad track for about 1 mile, to reach some blue waymarkers on the right. Follow these to reach a gate at the end of the moor. Go through the gate and go slightly right, following more blue markers, to join another good track. Follow this downhill, going past a small plantation and then through a gate into a lane. The remains of Norton's Tower are on the hillside to your left. Go straight ahead with a wall, first on your left then on your right, to reach a green lane. Go along this to reach the main Skipton-Grassington road. Turn left along it for $^3/_4$ mile, as far as None-Go-Bye Farm. There go left along a footpath marked 'Embsay'. Keep straight ahead to reach a footpath sign on your right. There take the path across an old railway line, going past Hoggs Farm, then Clark House and Oddacres Farm to enter the farmyard of Hill Top Farm over a stile. The way ahead is in front of two farm houses, through a gate and down a slope to cross a dam bank. On joining the road ahead turn right, along it, back into Embsay, so ending a super walk.

REFRESHMENTS:
The Elm Tree Inn, Embsay (tel no: 0756 790717).
None along the route.

Walk 81   ELGAR WAY CIRCULAR   13m (21km)

Maps: OS Sheets Landranger 98; Outdoor Leisure 2 & 10.

Moderate walking on limestone with some stiff climbs.

Start: 'Ye Olde Naked Man' café, Market Place, Settle.

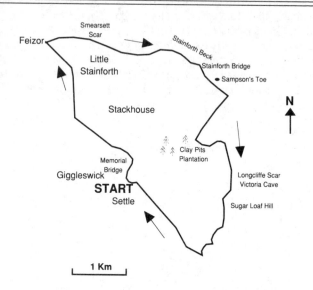

This route was devised by WR Mitchell, ex-editor of The Dalesman, to link places associated with Edward Elgar. Go up Bishopdale Court, left of 'Ye Olde Naked Man', and turn right along Kirkgate passing, on your right, **Victoria Hall**. Go under the viaduct and into Church Street. Turn left by Ribble Terrace and cross the riverside park to Kings Mill. Turn right and cross Giggleswick Memorial Bridge (built in 1982) over the Ribble. Turn left, then half-right along a tarmac path into Giggleswick. Turn right along Bankwell Road, then right again up **Belle Hill** where you cross the Abs. Go along The Mains, at the far end of which turn left along a lane, uphill, and go over a stile at the top. Bear right, going diagonally up a steep track and continue close to the quarry on your left. Follow yellow waymarkers to a signpost and turn right along Giggleswick Scar. Cross two stiles and bear half-right across a pasture to a signposted gate. Go half-right over two more stiles. Pass a bridleway signpost and take a rutted track down to

Feizor hamlet. Turn right near a bungalow and leave Feizor over a stile signposted 'Stainforth 1¹/₂ miles'. Climb a sunken way along a wall, right. Cross a stile in the wall and continue uphill on a green track over a pass. Go down the winding track into Little Stainforth and cross the road. Go down the narrow road to **Stainforth Bridge.** A stile, right, offers a 300 yard detour downstream to beautiful Stainforth Force. Cross the bridge and follow the narrow road uphill and over the Settle-Carlisle line, to the B6479. Cross and turn right, then left into Stainforth village, leaving it along steep Goat Scar Lane. At the lane end cross the stile, left, and go down a field to magnificent 60ft Catrigg Force. Return to the lane and cross the stile at its end into a large pasture. Turn right to a stile signposted 'Winskill ¹/₂ mile'. Go half-right then bear left along a narrow walled enclosure. Cross another stile and go right to join a farm road, passing 'Sampson's Toe', a Silurian boulder. At a T-junction go right for a mile to where the road goes right, downhill, and turn left along a gated track with Clay Pits Plantation on your right. Go past a barn and immediately after passing through a metal gate turn right over a stile signposted 'Stockdale Lane 1¹/₂ miles'. Follow a rough track between a wall, right, and Langcliffe Scar, left. Soon Victoria Cave is reached, half-way up the Scar. A detour to this archaeological site is recommended. Return to the track and continue along it to a stile on your right. Cross and go ahead with a wall, left, and Altermire Scar, right, to a stile on the left. Cross and bear right, uphill, to go around the shoulder of Sugar Loaf Hill, left, to enter Stockdale Lane. Turn right to High Hill Lane. Turn left for 800 yards to lovely Scaleber Force, a 40ft fall in a wooded ravine. Retrace your steps to signposted B R Mitchell lane on your left. Take it to join the old coach road and follow it to Settle.

POINTS OF INTEREST:

Victoria Hall – Dr CW Buck, a friend of Elgar's used to conduct the local orchestra in this Hall. He was born in the adjoining house.

Belle Hill – 'Brauendale' was Dr Buck's home and was frequently visited by Elgar.

Stainforth Bridge – A 17th century packhorse bridge, a firm favourite with Elgar.

The view from Goat Scar Lane over the roofs of Stainforth to Pot Scar and Smearsett Scar was painted and displayed on countless pre-war railway holiday posters.

REFRESHMENTS:

The Craven Heifer, Stainforth (tel no: 07292 2599).

Pubs, cafés and hotels in Settle.

Maps: OS Sheets Landranger 104; Pathfinder SE 25/35.

A tremendously varied short walk, going from the town centre to open countryside.

Start: At 293557, The Valley Gardens, Harrogate.

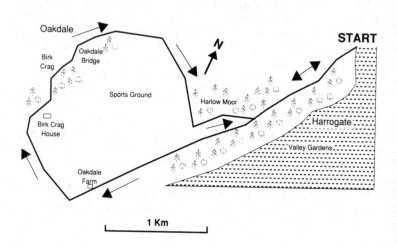

From **Harrogate** town centre enter the Valley Gardens through the main gates. Follow the left-hand path alongside the stream, recently named the 'Elgar Walk' to commemorate the composer's frequent visits to the town. At 'Bogs Field', site of no less than thirty-six different mineral springs, take the path that runs to the right of the tennis courts. On reaching the woods, take the second of two paths to your right, signposted 'Harlow Carr Gardens'. Follow the path through the pinewoods to Harlow Moor Road. Cross this road, and a few yards to the left follow a path signposted 'Crag Lane, Harlow Carr Gardens'. Indistinct at first, this path goes through woodland and then passes along the right-hand edge of a grassy clearing to join a metalled path. As this path reaches Crag Lane **Harlow Carr Botanical Gardens** is in front of you. If you wish to visit the gardens, the entrance is 50 yards to the left; otherwise follow the road to your right.

The road soon becomes a stony path and eventually veers right. After about 10 yards follow the footpath sign to the left, marked 'Cornwall Road'. You are now at the top of Birk Crag. Ahead, across the valley, is Queen Ethelburga's School, and slightly to the left is the Army Apprentice's College with its unusual pyramid-shaped chapels. The path follows the top of the crag and then falls steeply in a series of rough steps. Follow these to the left. After the first set of steps, ignore the path directly ahead and turn sharp left down a further flight. At the foot of the steps the path begins to rise slightly, and runs parallel with Oak Beck. After approximately 100 yards take the rough wooden steps to your left down to the beck, and then continue right along the bank to the bridge on Cornwall Road. Turn right and follow the road until you see the pinewoods to your left. The first path through them will take you back into the Valley Gardens.

POINTS OF INTEREST:

Note: The Valley Gardens are taken over for a few days in spring by the annual flower shows. The Tourist Information Centre (tel no: 0423 525666) will have the dates.

Harrogate – A spa town famous for its beautiful gardens, elegant Victorian architecture and fine conference and shopping facilities. At the Pump Room Museum, close to the entrance to the Valley Gardens, you can discover Harrogate's past and taste the waters which brought fame and prosperity to the town.

Harlow Carr Botanical Gardens – Beautiful surroundings in which to learn more about the art of gardening or simply to enjoy a relaxing stroll. As well as a variety of gardens there are an alpine house, arboretum and woodland walks with stunning display of rhododendrons (tel no: 0423 565418).

REFRESHMENTS:

The Harrogate Arms Hotel, Crag Lane (tel no: 0423 502434).
The Magnesia Well Café, Valley Gardens (tel no: 0423 525149).
Betty's, Parliament Street, (tel no: 0423 564659). Yorkshire's most famous tearooms!

Walk 83   HAMPSTHWAITE AND CLINT   4m (6.5km)

Maps: OS Sheets Landranger 99 & 104; Pathfinder SE 26/36 & 25/35.

An interesting walk with lots of history.

Start: The village green, Hampsthwaite.

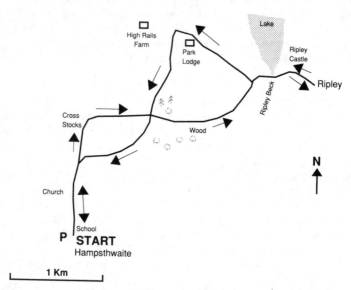

Walk towards Clint. Continue down the road passing **St Thomas à Becket church** and go over the bridge to a sharp right-hand bend in the road. The route goes straight ahead through a gate and climbs up the steep hill with a hedge on the right. Do stop and enjoy the splendid view into the valley of the Nidd. Go over stiles on to the road with the tiny hamlet of **Clint** to your left. Turn right along the lane marked with a dead end sign and follow it for about $1/2$ mile to a gate leading into Hollybank Wood. Meander through this lovely wood along the path over a bridge spanning Ripley Beck. At this point you have a good view of **Ripley Castle** and the lake. The way now takes you into the picturesque cobbled square of this old market town.

Leaving Ripley along the same path by which you entered the village. Go down over the beck to a fork junction. Turn right and keeping the wall on your right, follow a track, passing Sadler Carr Farm, Alicia Wood and Park Lodge all to the left. Before you come to High Rails Farm there is a junction: go left through the gate and straight ahead over the fields on a well-defined bridle path meeting up with the road where you entered Hollybank Wood. Cross the road and go down the bridle path linking up with the main road back to **Hampsthwaite** village.

POINTS OF INTEREST:

St Thomas à Becket church – Founded in 1180. There are several grave covers in the porch which indicate that a church existed in early Norman times. The church contains the tomb of Amy Woodforde Linden, composer of the *Indian love lyrics*. The porch was erected to the memory of William Makepeace Thackeray.

Clint – Beside the road you will see the remains of an old corpse cross.

Ripley Castle – The castle has been the residence of the Ingilby family for 650 years. It is open to the public from May to September on Sundays and Bank holidays.

Hampsthwaite – An ancient settlement of the Brigantes, it was the site of an important river crossing in Roman times.

REFRESHMENTS:

Ripley village has a café and tea shop.

Walk 84   KNOX MANOR AND SMELTHOUSES   4¹/₂m (7km)

Maps: OS Sheets Landranger 99; Pathfinder SE 06/16.

A nice easy walk with superb views and historical interests.

Start: At 191640, in the lane adjacent to Knox Manor. NOT in the restaurant's private car park.

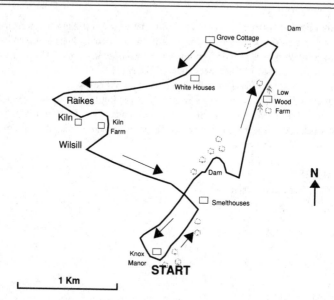

Follow the lane at the eastern side of Knox Manor through the wood to **Smelthouses**. Turn left over the bridge and almost immediately join the track on your right, signposted 'Whitehouses', that winds through the wood before descending to the side of Fell Beck. Walk upstream and cross over the wooden bridge above a small dam. Bear right, uphill, for 80 yards but then do not go past the building on your right. Instead turn sharp left on to a narrow path leading to a stile in the stone wall. Keeping to the general line of the beck, but on top of the escarpment, reach the walled green lane near Low Wood Farm.

Cross over the lane to the stile opposite and go through the small copse to an opening in the next wall, partially hidden by a large holly tree. On entering the field bordered by an indistinct sunken green track, bear left downhill and cross Fell Beck over a wooden bridge below the dam. Go over a wooden stile and proceed uphill for 70 yards along the farm track before turning left over the cattle grid into a field. Go forward along the track to Grove Cottage. Go over the stile at the left of the cottage and turn left along the lane towards Whitehouses. When you reach a junction with another lane coming from the right, cross straight over to the gate opposite which gives access to a green track meandering westwards roughly parallel to the main road above.

Continue along the track which exits on to a steep metalled road. At a sharp bend turn left down the road to Raikes and join the narrow path between two properties on the left that will take you to Kiln. Keep to the north-east side of the buildings at Kiln, bear left up the farm road and then sharp right at the junction. Pass Kiln Farm and continue down the road. Turn left along the road towards Smelthouses, but instead of crossing the bridge to rejoin the lane to Knox Manor, take the footpath on the right alongside one of the houses into the field above the beck. Follow the beck downstream and join the farm drive from Old Wall House back to Knox Manor.

POINTS OF INTEREST:
Smelthouses – The cottages are a picture in springtime and summer. This was the location of the earliest flax mill in Nidderdale established in 1798. As its name suggests there was a lead smelting mill there in the middle of the 14th century.

Walking towards Grove Cottage turn round, you will see all the mystical shapes of the famous Brimham Rocks.
From Whitehouses to Raikes you have a superb view of Guisecliffe with Yorkes Folly on the right.

REFRESHMENTS:
The Royal Oak, Dacre (tel no: 0423 780200). Welcome walkers.
The Darley Mill, (tel no: 0423 780857), on the B6451.

Walk 85   THE CHEVIN FOREST PARK   5m (8km)

Maps: OS Sheets Landranger 104; Pathfinder SE 24/34.

A walk up and along the moderately steep Chevin hillside. Mostly through woodland, using fairly good tracks and paths.

Start: The car park opposite the Church of All Saints', Otley.

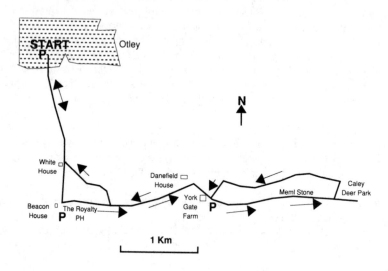

Walk south down nearby Station Road towards The Chevin. Cross the footbridge over the by-pass at the end of the road. Walk uphill to a minor road, and up the footpath opposite signposted Yorkgate. Cross a second road, go over a stone stile and continue up steps. To the right is the **White House**. Keep to the path uphill and through woodland until open land is reached near to the top. The hardest part of the walk is now over. A little higher, reach a wide track close to the Royalty Inn. Turn left along the track and eventually reach a gate with a stile on its right. Go through and follow the track down to the road at Danefield House.

Almost opposite, cross the stile and take a narrow footpath which runs uphill, parallel to the road, to reach a car park. Turn left along the track and bear right at a junction. A plaque informs us that the lime tree here was planted in memory of Thomas

Chippendale, and we now follow Chippendale Ride through the woodland. Ignore all tracks at the side as you cross a small stream and walk steadily eastwards. If the main track is muddy, a narrow footpath just below can be used. Reach the edge of the wood at a junction of several tracks and turn left downhill towards wooden electricity poles. Divert a short distance to the right along the path here to enjoy the views above Caley Crags. Return and follow the path west. You are now on part of the **Ebor Way**.

Reach more crags and bear slightly left above them as a path descends to the right. Re-enter woodland and cross a footbridge over a stream on which there are small waterfalls. Go up steps and bear right along a grass track. Before long this bears left and continues up to the car park previously visited. Retrace your steps along the path, now going downhill, to the stile. Cross the road by Danefield House, walk up the track to a gate and walk a short distance ahead on a track. You reach some isolated gateposts on your left: a signpost here indicates the path bearing right, downhill, back to the White House. Just before this, the steps used earlier are reached. Turn right, downhill, and retrace your steps along the easy-to-follow path to the footbridge, Station Road, **Otley** and the start.

POINTS OF INTEREST:
The White House – An information centre and tearooms. (Open 1–5pm April–October, 1–4pm November and December, Saturday and Sunday.)
The Ebor Way – A long distance path from Helmsley to Ilkley.
Otley – The home of Thomas Chippendale, carpenter supreme. Just south of the church, there is an excellent clock tower in the Market Place.

REFRESHMENTS:
Easily found in Otley from cafés and inns.

Walk 86   UPPER WASHBURN VALLEY   5m (8km)

Maps: OS Sheets Landranger 104; Pathfinder SE 05/15.

An easy walk, visiting the partly-submerged remains of what was once a thriving, water-powered textile-manufacturing community.
Start: At 154574, Thruscross Reservoir car park.

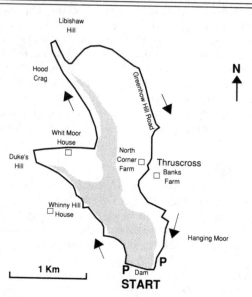

From the car park at the west end of the dam, cross the road and go through the gate opposite on to a permissive path. The path heads towards the reservoir, then follows the woodland edge near the water. At the first large inlet, turn left for a few yards along the former road, then right down a flight of steps to a footbridge. The path returns to the reservoir and proceeds north-west, but on reaching another former road you again turn left, then right, to regain the water's edge. Approaching the next inlet you follow the waymarks left through the wood, then right down steps to another bridge. The path now follows the western arm of the reservoir, fed by Capelshaw Beck, and on reaching yet another drowned road you make the usual left then right turn off the road, following the waymarks. The narrow ribbon of reservoir at this point corresponds to a valley which was dammed here to provide a head of water for Patrick's

Mill. A little further along, you reach the substantial ruins of Little Mill, which had two 18ft waterwheels. The path follows the watercourse which fed them: you can see the dam in this case by crossing the stile on to the road and following it right to the bridge which is built on it.

Climb the hill beyond and turn right for Scaife Hill. Pass in front of the house, go through the left-hand gate, and take a straight line across three fields to a stile at the north-west corner of Whit Moor House. Keep to the north side of this farm, then go straight ahead to find the ruins of stoutly-built Holme Field Head. Turn left here and walk for nearly a mile, first along the edge of the wood, then descending gently to cross a footbridge under Libishaw Scar. Turn right after crossing the stream and follow it down to a stile on the left where the wood begins. The stile leads to a narrow valley which you ascend, keeping well up on the left-hand side when there is no clear path. At the head of the little valley turn right, keeping above the marshy area, then make for the left-hand end of the ridge some distance away. Emerge on to the road, either through the gate or over the stile 150 yards further on. From the stile, turn right along the road for 500 yards, leaving it, right, when approaching a dip in the road, over a stile by a gate. Follow the left-hand wall and at the next gate turn half-left to another gate, where you continue in the same direction to a stile. Aim now for the left-hand side of the barn ahead, where you pass through a gate and turn left to the road-end at Thruscross Green. Head due south across the Green to find a stile. Cross and continue in the same line until the ground starts to fall. Follow the left-hand wall here as it turns left, descending gently. Keep just below the wall and, later, the hedge, but turn right just before a stone building to a gate by the Sailing Club. As you emerge on to the Club's private road turn left, then fork right along a grassy track which brings you to the public road. Turn right and follow the road back to the dam, or, by going left for nearly $^1/_2$ mile, to the Stonehouse Inn.

POINTS OF INTEREST:
The industrial hamlet of West End had been depopulated for many years before the valley was flooded in 1965.

REFRESHMENTS:
The Stonehouse Inn, (tel no: 094388 226).

Walk 87   **DACRE BANKS**   5m (8km)

Maps: OS Sheets Landranger 99; Pathfinder SE 06/16.

A varied walk over fields and moor and through woodland, with an easy climb.

Start: At 195616, in School Lane, Dacre Banks.

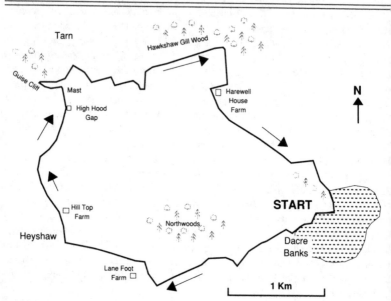

Pass the Youth Hostel at the end of School Lane and cross the cattle grid on to the farm road. Turn left uphill at the junction just past the bridge and walk through the farmyard to join a green track that begins at the left-hand side of large slurry tank. Follow this track uphill as it bends to the right and turn left through the second gateway. Continue with the wall on your left to the wooden stile in the perimeter fence of the second field. Climb over the stile in the stone wall ahead. Bear right across the middle of this next field, walking uphill towards the gate at the top leading on to a rough lane. Continue up to the crossroads. Turn right toward **Heyshaw**, passing the entrance to **Lane Foot Farm** on the left.

At the bottom of the lane go through the wooden gate and pass between the two buildings to reach a metal gate. Go through into a field and continue beside a fence on your left where you will soon discover signs of an old paved way. These stone slabs lead to a narrow gate. Pass through the adjoining, wide gateway and follow the paved path towards the farm at the top of the field. Bear to the right of the silage bay to a stile on to the lane at Heyshaw. Walk up the lane, turn right along the lane rough track towards Guise Cliff and go through the wooden gate on to Heyshaw Moor.

Follow the moorland road to the Telecom mast on the skyline. Bear left round the mast, go over the stile near the wall and, following the wall on the right, go through the small gap on to **Guise Cliff**. From this point there are splendid views back along the dale to Great Whernside and eastward to Brimham Rocks and the Hambleton Hills beyond. In the woods below is tiny Guise Cliff Tarn and many more delightful paths to explore for those who have time to spare. From the top of Guise Cliff follow the right-hand track down to wire fencing. Turn right along the track to a stile. Go straight ahead to another stile, turn left down the field, along the bottom to a stile in the wall on the left by a gate and follow the wall down to a stile in the corner. Follow the track through Hawkshaw Gill Wood. At the T-junction turn right and at the fork junction turn right again. Go up to and through a gate, along a field and through another gate to a gate next to the farm house of **Harewell House Farm**. Keep left through the farm and go down the farm lane. Keep right at the junction by the stream to return to School Lane.

POINTS OF INTEREST:

Heyshaw and Lane Foot Farm – Between these two you will find evidence of an old causeway or causey. The causeway was made with large stone slabs for a horse or mule, with the solid wheels of the carts riding on the ground on either side. No doubt an interesting sight in wet weather with a load of lead aboard!

Guise Cliff – An excellent spot to take a breather with fine views of the river Nidd, tiny hamlets and villages. The hamlet of Wisill is the site of one of the earliest settlements. Take care with children, there are steep drops.

Harewell House Farm – For gardening enthusiasts. I am sure the owner will be delighted to show you around, certainly worth a visit.

REFRESHMENTS:

The Royal Oak Inn, Dacre Village (tel no: 0423 780200). Walkers and children welcome.

The Darley Mill, B6451 to Harrogate Road (tel no: 0423 780857).

Walk 88   BURTON LEONARD TO BREARTON   5¹/₂m (9km)

Maps: OS Sheets Landranger 99; Pathfinder SE 26/36.

A pleasant and easy walk.

Start: The Green in Burton Leonard.

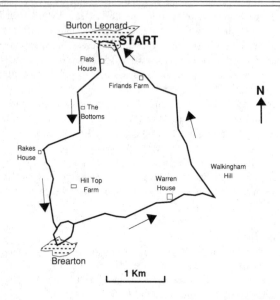

From the Green take the west road out of the village, past the telephone box and up the hill alongside the Top Green. Half-way up the hill turn left across the Green and into Scara Lane, past Meadow Court and Flats House. Just beyond this point turn right into the Lime Kilns Lane. About ¹/₄ mile further on the lane splits: take the left fork past the Nature Reserve and down to the Lime Kilns Beck. Cross the footbridge and take the track rising to a gate and the junction with Riggs Lane. Turn right into the lane and continue uphill past a wood on the left to a gate at the top of the hill. Dogs must be on leads here. Go through the gate and down the bridle path to Brearton village. On nearing the village the track meets Lillygate Lane and splits two ways: the left fork continues the walk, the right is slightly further but does take in the village. Assuming the right turn is made follow the lane to its junction with the main (only) street opposite the Malt Shovel. Turn left to the village green and pond, passing to the left of the green along the lane to its junction with Lillygate Lane once more. Follow the tarmac road to the right, past the gate to Hill Top Farm on the left, and on for approximately 1 mile. At a renovated farm on the left the lane then runs out to a grass track beyond a white double gate. Go through the gate and straight across the field, keeping a wood on the left and telephone poles on the right, to a wicket gate.

Beyond the gate turn sharp left and up a steep and sometimes slippery slope with a stone wall on the left and a wood on the right. Eventually the narrow track widens out to a bridle path and starts to fall downhill. Reach Jonty Beck, and a bridge over it. At this point Riggs Lane joins from the left. Cross the bridge and go up the lane on the other side to the Toll House which stands at the old turnpike point. Turn left past Firlands Farm and go back to Burton Leonard past the Royal Oak.

REFRESHMENTS:
There are no cafés but there is an excellent pub in each village.
The Royal Oak, Burton Leonard (tel no: 0765 87332).
The Malt Shovel, Brearton (tel no: 0423 862929).
The Hare & Hounds, Burton Leonard (tel no: 0765 87355). At present closed but due to re-open shortly.

Walk 89   **LINTON** $5\frac{1}{2}$m (9km)

Maps: OS Sheets Landranger 104; Pathfinder SE 24/34.

An easy walk, through farmland, between two pretty villages.

Start: At 390468, The Windmill public house, Linton.

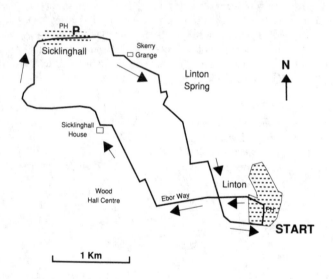

From **Linton** follow the road opposite the Windmill pub, Trip Lane, towards the Wood Hall Centre, then take the second footpath on the right, signposted 'Bridleway, Sicklinghall, Ebor Way'. The path passes through a copse for a few yards, follows the right-hand boundary of the field and then goes through another copse and along a stony lane. When you reach the drive to Sicklinghall House follow it to the right for 100 yards and then go through the white gates on the left (no footpath sign here). After 1 mile take the path on your right, clearly indicated by yellow waymarks from this point. Turn right at the main road and follow it through the village of **Sicklinghall**.

Continue up the hill to Linton Springs Farm and take the path on the right around the farm buildings and on to open land. After $\frac{1}{2}$ mile the paths turns left, and then right after a further 200 yards. When you reach the metalled lane of your original route, cross over and take the path straight ahead towards the river Wharfe. At the bottom of this path turn left along a road that overlooks the river. When you reach the main road, turn left to return to your starting point.

POINTS OF INTEREST:
Linton and Sicklinghall – Both well worth exploring for their delightful cottage architecture.

REFRESHMENTS:
The Windmill, Linton (tel no: 0937 62938).
The Scots Arms, Sicklinghall (tel no: 0937 62100).

Walk 90   HOOTON PAGNELL   6m (10km)

Maps: OS Sheets Landranger 111; Pathfinder SE 40/50.
Gentle walking in very pleasant countryside in the midst of a coal mining area.
Start: The church, Hooton Pagnell.

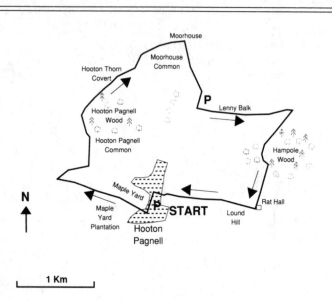

Alternative parking, and start, is possible on the grass verge of North Field Road.

From the church walk past the entry to Hooton Pagnell Hall. Cross the stile on the opposite side of the road and walk down the stone steps. Walk along the crop boundary towards the right-hand side of a small group of trees and continue ahead to reach Mapple Yard Plantation. The clear footpath through the wood commences at the left-hand side of the corner of a small drain. Cross the open field reached, to the right of an overgrown ditch, and bear slightly left over a footbridge. Continue ahead and go through a gap in the hedge and across the corner of the next field to reach a road. Turn right and follow the road past a track leading to the disused railway, and pass through the next gate on the left. Follow the track to Hooton Pagnell Wood. Do not enter, but turn left along the footpath at its edge. Keep on this as you pass the disused railway and go up to the next corner. Here, walk ahead to the left of a hedge and follow this to reach an open field. Bear a little left towards the right of a house to reach a road.

Turn left, then right at the road junction to go along Moorhouse Lane. A little before reaching a farm, turn right along a footpath on the right-hand side of a fence going slightly uphill and into an open field. Maintain direction across this to reach North Field Road. Turn right and walk to a gate on the left and enter the enclosed track, Lenny Balk. Reach a junction of tracks and turn left along the byway. Quickly bear right along a bridleway. This goes towards a hedge corner which may be easier reached along the field boundary. Continue along the left of the hedge and maintain this direction to reach a track. Turn right along this to Hampole Wood. The track follows the western edge to reach a corner, and enters the wood. At a junction turn left, slightly uphill. Just past an open area take the narrow footpath on the right, between trees, to reach a stile. Take the track ahead to Rat Hall Farm. Pass the farmhouse side and turn right in front of it, between buildings, along a field side to enter the enclosed lane, Narrow Balk. At its end, turn left and quickly right, along the wide footpath between houses to reach the B6442 road in **Hooton Pagnell**. Turn left to reach the church.

POINTS OF INTEREST:

Hooton Pagnell – A pleasant, largely stone built medieval village. All Saints' Church is nicely set on a mound. The adjacent hall has an interesting entrance and there is a tithe barn inside its grounds. Frickley Colliery is close to the route. It adds interest and does not intrude for long.

REFRESHMENTS:

No refreshments are available nearby.

Walk 91 BURTON LEONARD TO BISHOP MONKTON 6m (10km)
Maps: OS Sheets Landranger 99; Pathfinder SE 26/36.
An easy walk between two pleasant villages.
Start: The Green in Burton Leonard.

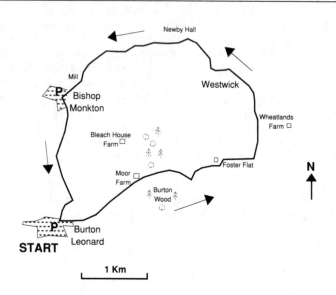

From the Green take the road east, past the Post Office and out of the village past the Hare and Hounds pub. Continue for $\frac{1}{4}$ mile to a crossroads. Cross the road and go down the lane past the 'No Through Road' sign. Moor Farm can now be seen $\frac{1}{2}$ mile ahead at the bottom of the lane. On reaching the farm skirt around to the right of the large green building and take the chalk stone road through a gate and down to the plantation approximately $\frac{1}{4}$ mile ahead. When nearing the plantation ignore the gate and lane to the left and follow the lane straight ahead, through the gate into the plantation. After approximately 100 yards, and after going through another gate, the lane ends into a field. Walk diagonally left across the field until Hol Beck is reached. Walk downstream to the bridge, cross over and go diagonally left to a stile over the fence. Go over the stile and up the field, with the hedge on your right, to Foster Flatts

Farm. Skirt the farm on the right to reach the road to Roecliff Corner $^1/_4$ mile ahead. On reaching the main road turn left to Bishop Monkton.

Follow the road for about $2^1/_2$ miles into Bishop Monkton with its two pubs and a stream running along the main street. Follow the stream to the church and cross over the road into Church Farm. Keep left in the farmyard, with caravans on the right, and go over a stile. Keeping the hedge on the left, walk to the next stile. Go over and straight across the meadow to another stile in a hedge. Beyond this stile is a low bank: go up into a field. With the hedge again on the left, follow the edge of the field for 100 yards to a stile in the corner which can be missed if care is not taken. Go over the stile and across a ploughed, but well trodden, field to a stile into a meadow. When in the meadow head for the double-legged power pole. On reaching the pole go through the gate behind, and follow a lane to a large house surrounded by trees. Passing the house on your left continue down the lane to its junction with Straight Lane. Turn right, pass St Cuthbert's Church on the right, and walk back to the Green.

Please note that all the stiles mentioned in the second part of the walk are marked with a large arrow which can be seen from a considerable distance.

REFRESHMENTS:

The Royal Oak, Burton Leonard (tel no: 0765 87332).
The Hare & Hounds, Burton Leonard (tel no: 0765 87355).
The Mason's Arms, Bishop Monkton (tel no: 0765 87322).
The Lamb & Flag, Bishop Monkton (tel no: 0765 87427).

Walk 92   **BLUBBERHOUSES**   7m (12km)

Maps: OS Sheets Landranger 104; Pathfinder SE 05/15.

A straightforward, interesting walk.

Start: At 553168, the layby below the church at Blubberhouses.

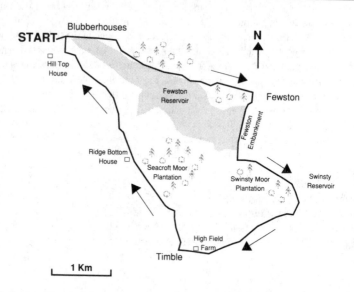

Walk along and up the hill, on the main road towards Harrogate, to Hopper Lane layby.
At the top of the layby go over the stile into the wood and, follow the track, keeping
to the right, down and along the edge of the reservoir. Keep walking until you come to
the end, by a fence. Here turn left through the gate into a wood. Go through the wood
to a minor road. Turn right, passing the school on your left. A little way on, go through
the gap into the woodland on your right. Go through to another minor road. Turn right,
following the road over the Fewston Embankment to the Swinsty Moor Plantation and
National Trust car park. Go through the wicket gate by the 'Public Footpath' sign, and
through the trees of Swinsty Moor Plantation, to arrive at ancient Swinsty Hall. Bearing
right, follow the track up through the wood to a gate into a field. Walk straight ahead,
up two fields over stone stiles, then bear slightly left across a field to a wooden stile.
Follow the wall to a gate with a wall stile near it. You will now enter a walled track,

keep to the right. Pass two lovely old 1683 and 1668 houses, and reach Timble.

If you turn right Timble Inn is just a short walk down the road, but the route follows the sign to Blubberhouses. At the sign go over the stile by the iron gate and walk ahead through a walled enclosure. Go straight up the field, through the gate on the right and down a field to a stile in the corner, with a wooden plank. Walk diagonally to the left over the next field to a gate to a minor road. Cross and enter the wood by the Blubberhouse sign. Take the middle track through the wood. Keeping to the right, you will come to a track road. Go over this into a wood. Go down to a wooden bridge over a stream, then on to a stone stile. Walk ahead to enter a green lane: follow this and go over a fence stile. The track bears right, then left through gateposts to an iron gate stile. Make towards the trees to reach a stile in the wall. Keep on the left track through the field, with the wall on your right and go over the stone stile by a tree. Now, with the wall on your left, go ahead over a wooden stile and keep left to a stone stile in the corner. Follow the wall to a wooden stile. Go over and down the fields, with the little church to your left, and over a stile back to your car.

REFRESHMENTS:
In Fewston there is a vegetarian tea shop which is well worth a visit.

Walk 93   SHAW MILLS TO RIPLEY   7m (12km)

Maps: OS Sheets Landranger 99; Pathfinder SE 26/36.
A fine walk following a section of the Nidderdale Way.
Start: The Nelson Inn, Shaw Mills.

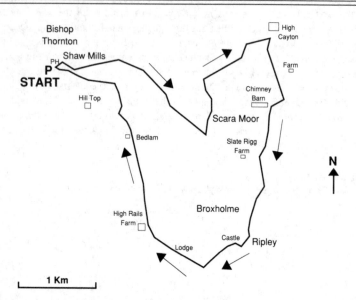

From the Nelson Inn walk along the road towards Ripon. At the last house in the village
the road turns sharp left: leave the road and cross over three stiles, very close together,
into a field. Walk across the field to a five-barred gate and a Nidderdale Way sign. Go
through the gate, turn half-left and climb diagonally up the field, to a stone wall and
another Nidderdale Way sign. Turn right and, with the wall on your left, walk down
towards marshy ground. The track rises sharply to farm buildings at the top of the hill.
Turn right at the farm and follow the track down through a single gate to Kettle Spring
Farm. Pass to the right of the buildings and out on to the farm lane. Follow the lane to
its junction with the main road. Turn left up the road for $^1/_2$ mile past a house in a wood
and then turn right at the Nidderdale Way sign into a lane with a plantation on the left.
Walk along the lane and down a single path with a plantation, on the right, to stepping
stones over Cayton Beck.

Cross the stones and pass through the gate on the right into the glen. Turn left and, with the fence of the wood on the left and marshy ground on the right, walk for ¹/₂ mile. There are several arrows on posts indicating the way to a gate in a stone wall. Pass through the gate and follow the edge of the wood on the right down past a small red brick building. Go through a gate and down the field. Go over an arched bridge and left to a gate into a wood. The path from the gate is narrow and can be very slippery after rain. Climb the path through the wood, following Nidderdale Way signs into Braithwaite Lane and down across the B6165 into Ripley.

From Ripley walk past the Castle (*see* Walk 83) and into Hollybank Lane. Go uphill, following a park wall. When the wall turns right, we leave the Nidderdale Way which carries on into the wood. Continue to follow the wall. Go over a stile, through a gate and over another stile. After this second stile the path veers away to the left. Leaving the wall to the right, cross the field diagonally to a post with an arrow. Follow the fence down over two gates. The main road can now be seen: follow the hedge on your right passing through the side garden of a recently renovated house and on to the road. Cross the road, known as Whipley Bank, and go into Law Lane. From here it is 1 mile of pleasant walking down to Shaw Mills.

REFRESHMENTS:

There are excellent tearooms at Ripley:

Butlers Pantry (tel no: 0423 770152). Open 10am to 5pm. Closed Friday.

Castle Tea Rooms (tel no: 0423 770152). Open 12 noon to 6pm. Closed Monday.

The Nelson Inn, Shaw Mills (tel no: 0423 770273). Bar snacks.

Walk 94   **Ripley to Cayton Ghyll**   7$\frac{1}{2}$m (13km)

Maps: OS Sheets Landranger 99; Pathfinder SE 26/36.

A pleasant, easy walk.

Start: The town square, Ripley.

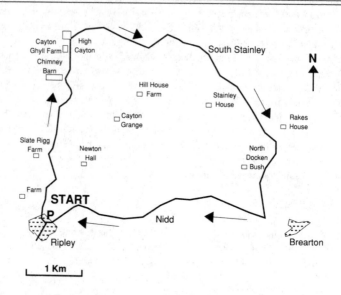

From the cobbled town square take the road north past the garage on the left, and Post Office on the right, towards the end of the town. Turn left past the tennis courts to follow a Nidderdale Way sign. Cross the B6165 road into Birthwaite Lane and follow it for $\frac{1}{2}$ mile to a sign for Slate Rigg Farm. At this point fork right along a grass track: a blue arrow on a yellow background marks the way. Follow the track past a plantation on the right. After a further 300 yards the Nidderdale Way turns right at a signpost and drops down a path through a wood to a gate. After the gate turn right down the field and over an arched bridge go across the beck. Go up the field to a gate with arrows. Go through and veer left past a small brick building on your left. Follow the contour of the hill, keeping the pine trees on the left, and go down to a gate in a stone wall. Follow the path towards marshy ground and, keeping the marsh to the left, continue for 400 yards until a tower with a water pump can be seen. At this point pass into the field with the tower and leave the Nidderdale Way. From the gate walk up the field to High Cayton Farm. Go through a mesh gate into the fold yard and out on to the farm road, which leads to South Stainley. Follow the track down to the A61, leaving Cayton Ghyll Farm and Cayton Grange on the right. Cross the A61 and walk down the side of the Red Lion pub into Stainley village. Go past St Wilfred's Church and out to Stainley Hall Farm. Leaving the farm on the left, cross the bridge over Stainley Beck and follow the track for $^3/_4$ mile to the junction with Riggs Lane. Follow the lane to the right down to Prince William Wood, on the left, and Docken Bush Whin, on the right. Shortly after this reach the Brearton to Nidd road. Turn right towards Nidd and follow the road into the village. Just before the village, turn right over a disused railway bridge and walk to the junction with the A61. Cross and walk south $^1/_2$ mile to **Ripley** and the start of the walk.

POINTS OF INTEREST:
Ripley – Outside the castle is All Saints' Church, with musket ball marks on the walls. said to have been caused by Oliver Cromwell's men. The old stocks stand in the town square.

REFRESHMENTS:
Butlers Pantry, Ripley (tel no: 0423 770152). 10am to 5pm. Closed Friday.
Castle Tea Rooms, Ripley (tel no: 0423 770152). 12 noon to 6pm. closed Monday.
The Red Lion, Stainley (tel no: 0423 884103).

Maps: OS Sheets Landranger 99; Pathfinder SE 26/36.
The longer version reaches Brimham Rocks, an interesting site.
Start: The Nelson Inn, Shaw Mills.

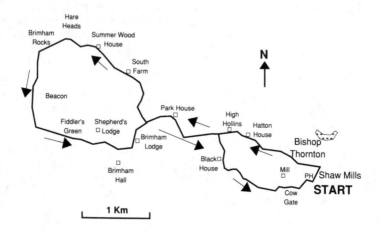

From Shaw Mills take the road to Bishop Thornton. At the top of Thornton Bank turn left into Cut Throat Lane past a 'No Through Road' sign. Continue down the walled lane to a small farm on the left and a stream with a footbridge. The lane is joined from the left by another track also coming up from Shaw Mills. Continue to follow the walled track to Hatton House Farm. Just past the farm the track becomes a chalk stone road. Approximately $\frac{1}{3}$ mile further, turn left on to a tarmac road. Another $\frac{1}{3}$ mile brings you to the Nidderdale Way coming in from the left at Black House. Continue to a cattle grid and ignoring the new road to the right, pass over the grid and down into the yard of the former Woodfield Mill. Pass the mill on your right and go through a gate to a Nidderdale Way sign pointing to the right across a field to a gap in a drystone wall on the left. Turn through the gap and follow a number of arrows down to a stream and a wood on the right. Cross the stream, and go through a gate up the field with a stone wall on the right. Go through three more gates, with the wall now on the left, to a T-junction at the third gate. At this point we turn right, leaving the Nidderdale Way and walk the 200 yards to Park House Farm. Turn left just before the farm and walk up to a gate into a meadow. Go through the gate and keeping the wall on the immediate left, climb up the field, go over two stiles and on to a track. Ignore the arrows the other side of the track and turn right along it: we have now regained the Nidderdale Way. Follow the track and Nidderdale Way signs to Brimham Rocks. The last part of the Way is a path across a peat and bracken moor which can be very boggy in the winter.

When reaching the road there is a choice of routes. Turn right to visit Brimham Rocks or turn left to continue a shorter walk.

To continue, turn left on the road and walk approximately 1 mile to a crossroads, passing Mauds Farm on the left. The Nidderdale Way slips off to the right, down to Smelthouses, part way along this section. Turn left at the crossroads and walk downhill towards Burnt Yates passing Fiddlers Green and Shepherds Lodge, both on the left. After about 1 mile the road turns sharp right. At this point leave the road and follow a lane straight ahead to Brimham Lodge Farm. Pass through the farm, with the house on the right, and down to the point at which we left the Nidderdale Way on the outward leg of the walk. Turn right and follow the original path past Woodfield Mill back to the sign which points to the right and down to Black House. Just before Black House turn left through a gate, down to Thornton Beck. Cross the footbridge and turn left to a stile over a drystone wall. Go over the stile and walk up the field to the wood side. Turn left and follow the wood to a track which in turn changes to a farm road. Ignore the arrows to the right which lead to Burnt Yates, and follow the track to Shaw Mills passing three farms along the way. The track eventually meets Pye Lane in Shaw Mills. Turn left over Pye Lane bridge and back to the Nelson Inn.

REFRESHMENTS:
Information Centre at Brimham Rocks, (tel no: 0423 780688). Teas at Weekends and Bank holidays.
The Nelson Inn, Shaw Mills (tel no: 0423 770273). Bar meals.

Walk 96   **ABERFORD**   9m (14.5km)

Maps: OS Sheets Landranger 105; Pathfinder SE 43/53.

Pleasant countryside with gentle walking.

Start: Park near the bridge in Aberford, or, if you don't wish to cross the A1, in a layby east of the Crooked Billet Inn.

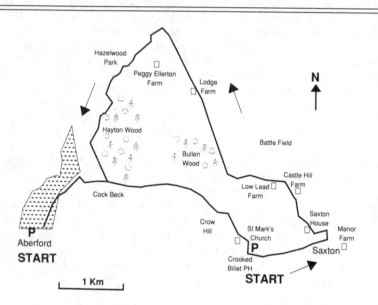

Walk north to the Arabian Horse Inn and bear right down Field Lane. This becomes a track before reaching the A1. Cross and continue along the track opposite, past a house and a field on the right. The wide track turns right towards a gate and stile. Later you will return to this point. If you are parked east of Aberford, exclude the route to here. Go through the gate, turn left on the clear track a little above a small stream and approach Cock Beck. Cross stiles to follow the path to the southern edge of Hayton Wood and bear slightly right close to the beck. Go along the wide area between fence and beck until you reach a fence ahead. Bear left upwards along the fence and go right at the top to meet a track. Turn right and soon pass through a gate before Lead Hall Farm. Cross the stile on the left, near the farm, and walk across the field to **Lead Church**. Continue to the B1217 just to the right of The Crooked Billet Inn.

194

Cross and go through the car park. Pass through a small gap in the hedge near to the eastern corner and follow the hedge side. Go straight across an open field to a gap in a hedge. Walk to the right of a large pylon and follow the waymarks on a series of telegraph posts to reach a gate at Saxton. Pass through a garden area to the road. Turn left to the church. Use the gate to the churchyard, and pass round the south and west sides of the church to Dam Lane. Turn left and, soon, right at a junction, to go along Milner Lane. Cross the B1217 and take the track opposite, past Castle Hill Farm.

Cross Cock Beck and continue along the track uphill past Low Lead Farm. Note **Castle Hill Wood** on the right. Pass a track junction on the left and turn right at the next to pass Newstead and Lodge Farms. Turn left at the junction towards **Hazelwood Castle** and left again towards Peggy Ellerton Farm. A stile on the right is soon reached. Follow the hedge and a wall down to a stile and bear right by an overgrown pond surrounded by trees. Emerge and turn left to a corner. Bear right across the field towards a copse. The path turns right and left before passing just inside the right-hand side of the copse. Cross over the field to a wide track and turn left towards Hayton Wood. Turn right along the side of the wood. Reach a corner of wood and field, and continue straight ahead across the open field to again reach the junction before Cock Beck. Retrace your steps to **Aberford**.

POINTS OF INTEREST:

Aberford – A pleasant village with several old buildings, one of the best of which is St Ricarius Church.

Lead Church – Dedicated to St Mary and still used a little. Very simple inside. The church is preserved with the help of various groups including the RA. Please sign the visitors book!

Castle Hill Wood – On the western flank of the Towton battlefield. Over 80,000 men fought here in Britain's biggest battle on Palm Sunday, 28 March, 1461. Half died and Cock Beck ran red with blood. Good views of the battlefield are seen to the east. A car journey to the cross on the B1217 takes you to the centre of the battlefield. A track here leads to good views of Cock Beck and Bloody Meadow.

Hazelwood Castle – A residential home. Note the large bells near to the entrance.

REFRESHMENTS:

Plentiful with three inns in Aberford and two in Saxton.

Walk 97   ABERFORD AND GARFORTH   9¼m (14.8km)
Maps: OS Sheets Landranger 105; Pathfinder SE 43/53.
An easy, interesting walk along paths and bridleways.
Start: The centre of Aberford.

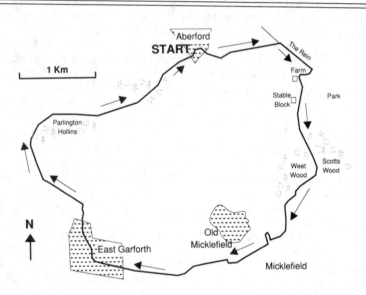

Go southwards along the main street and turn left into Lotherton Lane. Go under the A1 and turn left into a cul-de-sac with a through route for walkers. After ²/₃ mile, immediately beyond where a tree lined mound, The Rein, crosses the road, turn right through some large gates. Continue with the mound on your right for ¹/₂ mile to the next road. Turn right along its verge for 350 yards, then go left along a road signposted 'Sherburn-in-Elmet', passing Lotherton farm on your left. Continue to a house on the next corner. Turn right into the grounds of Lotherton Hall and go straight ahead between the Hall and the stable block. Continue along a flagged path to a kissing gate in the far corner of the gardens. Go along the right-hand side of the field ahead, then take a path across fields to a wood. Take a clear track through this, then turn right and keep close to its edge for ¹/₂ mile. At the far south-west corner turn left on a track across arable land for ¹/₂ mile to a T-junction of tracks. Turn right to the A1 and go right to cross it on a footbridge. Go left on a track which curves right to enter Old Micklefield. Cross the street to the right of the Blands Arms and go straight ahead, past a fish shop, to a track. Go along this, over fields, for $^1/_3$ mile to a T-junction. Turn right for 20 yards, then left, along a narrowing field path to reach a corner stile. Cross and continue in the same direction over the next field to another stile. Cross and go left along the verge of a Roman Road. After 100 yards go right, across it, and along a partly surfaced farm road. Where this curves towards the farm, continue ahead, close to a hedge on your left, to some houses. Pass these, keeping straight on past a bus roundabout, then going alongside a railway to the foot of a railway bridge. Turn right along a surfaced path for 300 yards to another road and turn left, briefly, into Harlech Way. Go along it to reach the first street on the left, and turn along it to allotments at the far end. Turn right to reach the Community Centre, then turn left along **Sturton Lane** to East Garforth Post Office. Cross the road, go down Ash Lane and, where it forks, go right. Turn left before a concrete works. After 30 yards bear right down a lane alongside the works, passing a house and keeping left of a low building ahead, to cross a stile in the left-hand corner. Cross the field diagonally left to a stile in a hedge and continue straight ahead to cross a footbridge in the next field. Turn left, along the edge of the field, to cross a corner stile near a copse. Turn half-right on to a path across a field to a stile. Continue ahead over the next field to a road and go along it for $^1/_4$ mile. Turn right into Parlington Lane and follow it for $2^1/_2$ miles to Aberford.

POINTS OF INTEREST:

The Rein – Part of a series of Iron Age earthworks spreading eastwards and westwards from Aberford.

Lotherton Hall – Started in the 1890s and finished during the Edwardian period. After only 60 years as a family home it was given to Leeds by Sir Alvary Gascoigne in 1968. Its 160 acres include formal gardens, a deer park and a bird garden.

Parlington Estate – For centuries, the home of the Gascoigne family. The date of the original house, long since demolished and of which little remains, is not known. But it was re-furbished in the 1730s. There are ponds, mature trees and a tunnel in the park, which is a mixture of woodland and arable farmland.

REFRESHMENTS:

There are several pubs in Aberford and Old Micklefield.

Walk 98   MICKLEFIELD CIRCULAR   10¼ m (16.4km)

Maps: OS Sheets Landranger 105; Pathfinder SE 42/52 & 43/53.
An easy walk through pleasant countryside.
Start: The Blands Arms, Old Micklefield.

From the Blands Arms take the track opposite the fish shop, eastwards, to the A1. Go left to bridge it, then right for 500 yards past the sewage works. Bear left on a clear field track under a railway bridge. Reach a wood, follow it briefly, then go right through it on a path to a level crossing. Keep on the path. Skirting a quarry to a path junction at a plantation. Do not go right, but continue ahead for 150 yards through the trees. Turn left along a path, then right about 15 yards from the wood edge. At the bottom corner of the wood turn right and descend . Turn left along a side road footpath to the Leeds-Selby road. Cross into a side road (the entrance to the Boot And Shoe car park). Go towards the pub, then right on a footpath across a field to a marker near a wood. Go through the wood to a stile. Cross parkland on a track marked by posts, going left through trees after 100 yards, to a stile in more woodland. Go through the wood to a track junction. Bear slightly left on a broad track to **Ledsham**. Walk through, turn right at the churchyard corner and, after 200 yards, take the second turn left near Grange Cottage – DO NOT continue into Manor Garth – along a lane which curves right and loses its surface. After $^1/_2$ mile go into a wood. Turn right on the next surfaced road for $^1/_2$ mile to the top of a rise where, opposite a farm lane on your right, turn left on a track to the left end of the farm ahead and on to a road at Newton Ings. Go right and right again at the second gateway, near a bus stop. Cross a stile and take a track past woods. Continue on a path near a hedge, left. Where this goes left go half-right to a stile in the far corner. Continue with a fence on your right to a road. Go right through Ledston to the village hall. Go left along Green Lane. Go past the school and on to the next road. Go right past Home Farm and up a slope. Go left after overhead wires, through a field, on a path to a road. Go left towards **Kippax** and first right towards a sports club. Go behind the club house to the end of the street beyond. Go forward between houses and turn left. Just past 51 Lime Tree Crescent go right on a track beside allotments. After 100 yards, where a path bears right, go ahead on the wider lane, with new housing on the left. Beyond, enter fields and turn left just before electricity wires. After 100 yards go right on a track to the main road. Go right, briefly, then cross at a footpath marker. Take this footpath away from the road. After 300 yards go half-right, crossing a large field to the 1st century AD Roman Road. Go left along it, cross a railway bridge and join a path on the right leading to a stile. Go over the field ahead to another stile in the corner. Keep to the edge of the next field. Where a track crosses your line of walk, go right on it for 20 yards, then left on a track to Micklefield.

POINTS OF INTEREST:

Ledsham – The church is probably the most complete Saxon church in West Yorkshire. The lower part of the tower, the nave and chancel arch are 8th century. The belfry is Norman and there are 15th century additions.

REFRESHMENTS:

The Blands Arms, Old Micklefield (tel no: 0532 862465).
The Boot and Shoe (tel no: 0977 682163).

Maps: OS Sheets Landranger 105; Pathfinder SE 43/53 & 44/54.
A pleasant, easy walk by wood and field paths.
Start: The main crossroads in the middle of Bramham village.

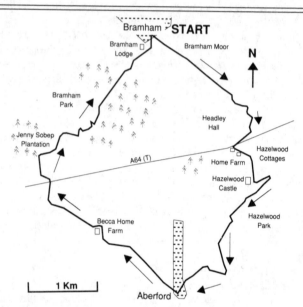

Go south-east along Fleely Lane towards Bramham Lodge and, on leaving the village, cross a road and continue along the one opposite. After $^3/_4$ mile this road becomes a dirt road for a further $^3/_4$ mile to where it meets a surfaced road at Headley Hall. Go between the buildings of Leeds University's farm to a facing, long building. Go right. The road bears left and, after 150 yards, you pass buildings and silos on the right. Just beyond, go right to the edge of a field. Go left on a track across the next field and immediately right down a field's edge to its bottom corner and a stile leading to the A64. Go right for 700 yards to a house on the left. There, cross the A64 and along a track, passing a lodge. After about 1 mile, at a side gate to Hazelwood Castle, turn left along an estate road. Pass the first entrance and continue for $^1/_4$ mile. Go right, briefly, along a lane signed "Peggy Ellerton Farm". Go right over a stile into a field and along its right side, crossing the front of **Hazelwood Castle**. At the end of the field cross a stile near the corner and take a faint path, passing a pond on your left, to arable land. Go left, briefly, and continue along a path going half-right towards trees on the skyline. Turn left just before them along a track that turns right to skirt trees. At the north-west corner of these go ahead, south-west, to a distant large tree near the remains of a stile with a sign. Go left along a track to the corner of a large wood. Turn right, edging it, for $^2/_3$ mile and at a sign go south, parallel to the wood, left, to reach and cross a stile in a fence. Continue ahead, across a field, close to a fence on the right to a stile short of a stream. Go right on a clear path. Cross another stile and go right, up a slope, to a track. Go left to the A1. Cross into a lane for Aberford. Cross the former Great North Road to a signed bridleway and go along it for $^3/_4$ mile, passing Becca Banks earthworks. Bear left with a wood on your left, leaving the main track, and edge a field to enter a lane leading to Becca Home Farm. About 20 yards past its last building, on the left, go left across a field to a bridge over a stream. Go left, briefly, then right, edging a field and the top edge of a wood. Continue along the left of the field ahead and cross a narrow wood. Edge the field ahead to a stile. Go half right crossing another field diagonally to a road north of Potterton. Go right to the A64. Go left, briefly, then right into a lane. After 600 yards go right at a stile near a wood. Continue for $^1/_3$ mile, crossing a dip. When the wood on your left ends turn right along a track to another wood and a short distance into it go right. Where the track splits, take the left fork for $^1/_2$ mile, edging a wood, to reach a temple. Pass this, edging the wood for 350 yards, then turn left along a track for a further 350 yards. Turn right along another track, going past Well Hill Farm to a road. Go right to the A1. Cross and follow the minor road back to Bramham.

POINTS OF INTEREST:
Hazelwood Castle – Built before 1286 because in that year Edward I gave permission for Sir William Vavasour to build a chapel there. In 1290 the family was given a licence to put up battlements.

REFRESHMENTS:
There are pubs in Bramham and Aberford.

Walk 100 PATELEY BRIDGE TO RAMSGILL   11$\frac{1}{2}$m (20km)

Maps: OS Sheets Landranger 99; Pathfinder SE 06/16 & 07/17.
A moorland walk partly around Gouthwaite reservoir.
Start: The High Street, Pateley Bridge.

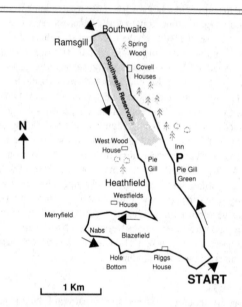

From the High Street walk down towards the River Nidd. At the bridge turn right to a footpath to Wath. After 100 yards the path passes to the left of a wooden building and then follows the river closely, it is never more than 100 yards away on the left, to Wath about $\frac{1}{2}$ hour away. For the most part the path is on the base of the old Nidderdale Light Railway which means it is well drained and offers good walking all year round. Cross a plank bridge over Wath Road, and follow the Nidderdale Way signs, keeping the river on the left, up to the wall of Gouthwaite Reservoir. Climb the path to the right and slightly away from the reservoir boundary fence to a hard, unmade road. Turn left on to this road and, with the reservoir on the left, continue for $1\frac{1}{2}$ miles to Bouthwaite village. At Bouthwaite leave the Nidderdale Way and turn left to Ramsgill $\frac{1}{2}$ mile away.

At Ramsgill turn left on to the road to Pateley Bridge and follow the road for about

2 miles to a point where a Nidderdale Way sign turns right up a very steep gated road to Heathfield Top. From Heathfield Top take the bridleway road to Moss Carr past the Leng House Hostel. Just past the hostel leave the track and follow the path down two fields, with the hedge on the right, to Spring House. Pass a farm and skirt the buildings on the right. Turn downhill to the caravan site which can be seen in the bottom of the valley. Turn right at the site and follow the road which runs alongside it. Ignore a small Nidderdale Way sign which points into the site and follow the road to a large Nidderdale Way sign which points to a chalk stone track between the caravans. Follow this gated track for approximately 1 mile, climbing all the way up to some old mine workings. At this point follow the Nidderdale Way, winding down to Brandstone Beck. Cross the beck and wind up through the spoil heaps. There is no established route to the top: the path that suits you best is the path to take and all paths end up on The Nab, the highest point, overlooking the old workings. With your back to the mine workings look at the skyline on which there is a drystone wall. In the wall is a wicket gate and 100 yards to the right of the gate, but not visible from The Nab, is a rough track which winds very slowly down to Hole Bottom and the lane to Roundhill Reservoir. Keep on this track, which has plenty of Nidderdale Way signs and which eventually becomes metalled, to Riggs House, on the right, and Ladies Riggs, on the left. Go on to Eagle House and the Pateley to Greenhow road. Turn left down the 1 in 6 hill to Bridgehouse Gate and back into Pateley Bridge High Street.

REFRESHMENTS:
There are plenty of cafés etc in Pateley Bridge.
The Sportsman Arms, Wath (tel no: 0423 771306). Meals.
The Yorke Arms, Ramsgill (tel no: 0423 75243).

TITLES IN THE SERIES